Skira Architecture Library

Luca Molinari

North American Architecture Trends 1990–2000

Introduction by
Adalberto Dal Lago

Skira

Editing
Emma Cavazzini

Layout
Sabina Brucoli

Translation from Italian
Antony Shugaar

*The first edition of this volume
has been published thanks
to Marazzi Gruppo Ceramiche SpA*

First published in Italy in 1999
by Skira Editore S.p.A.
Palazzo Casati Stampa
via Torino 61
20123 Milano
Italy

Printed and bound in Italy.
First edition

ISBN: 88-8118-865-1

Distributed in North America
and Latin America by Rizzoli
International Publications, Inc.
through St. Martin's Press,
175 Fifth Avenue, New York,
NY 10010, USA
Distributed elsewhere in the world
by Thames and Hudson Ltd.,
181a High Holborn,
London WC1V 7QW, United
Kingdom

Contents

Adalberto Dal Lago

Introduction

Despite the widespread interest in American architecture, from the immediate postwar period to the present day, this publication originated with the intent to constitute a solid contribution to the general understanding of a creative, productive, and cultural world that over the last decade has experienced an astounding acceleration, capable of influencing with its creations the international debate of the world of architecture.

The important thing is to note the elements of novelty and at the same time the traces of fine red thread that links several of the most important American design experiences with the aesthetic and cultural growth of the twentieth century, from Frank Lloyd Wright to Louis Kahn, all the way up to the works of Buckminster Fuller and Charles and Ray Eames.

A skillful and explosive blend of technological innovation, modernity, utopia, and social progress that has nourished American architecture, quickly transforming it into the modern architecture par excellence and into one of the standards by which to measure European and international production.

An attempt to plumb the complexities that characterize our reality and dig into the history of the more representative works of contemporary culture should be an emblematic effort on the part of a cultural enterprise that looks to reality as a sole, true point of reference and, at the same time, as a stimulus to change and evolve.

Indeed, for a major company, contemporary architecture should represent a significant metaphor through which to express its own corporate values.

A company that works in the field of construction cannot help but be extremely interested in the evolution of style, cultural sensibilities, and aesthetics. It must be creative, dynamic, and flexible. The important thing is to grasp and take part in the complex interweaving that goes on between the arts of vision and space and industrial applications.

Just as a high-tech company cannot remain indifferent to the scientific debate, likewise a company with a high creative content cannot fail to take an interest in architecture.

To publish right now *North American Architecture Trends 1999–2000* means interpreting an understanding of design activity as a structural constant that forms part, to all intents and purposes, of the economic dimension of a company; it means investing in the culture of design and planning, and in general maintaining a constant relationship with the most advance cultural research, not for a sort of ethical and psychological redemption toward society, but because economic value cannot be distinguished from a horizon that refers to a significance of understanding and intellectual excitement, unfailingly present even in the most mundane tools of the trade.

In this operation of institutional image, the creation of this volume clearly expresses a determination not to settle for ideological promises, but rather to work in concrete terms to make a corporate philosophy always compatible with the development of the cultural debate, translating this open approach into forms, structures, and material testimonials.

It means an awareness of the autonomy of design, it means respect for the creators of forms: form as communication, without ever forgetting the ultimate and fundamental destiny of images and objects, to be capable of speaking the language of function, transferring a unique and unrepeatable experience.

And, to echo the words of Louis Kahn, who wrote: 'the three chief desires of man are the desire to learn, the desire to communicate, and the desire to live well', we want to believe that the constant search for quality through the analysis of contemporary works can guide designers, companies, and public administrators in the construction of a contemporary culture that is finally built to the measure of man.

Luca Molinari

The American Nineties

A decade — no matter how fictitious such a chronological criterion may prove to be — can concentrate in itself a series of events and traces capable of describing the new phenomena, the elements of continuity and resistence, the actors involved and the context that surrounds them. A decade allows a historian and critic to maintain a slight distance from the press of events that submerges and makes valid everything only for the moment in which it is experienced.

Many of the cultural and artistic phenomena of recent years seem, in fact, to move schizophrenically from a generalized appeal to memory, as an ambiguous character split between the autobiographical and an idealized identification of the cultural and natural roots, and a lack of critical distance from the experiences in which we are immersed. As if the speed imposed by institutions, by the cultural industry, and the very tools utilized were no longer tolerable in terms of the natural times of the development and execution of the work.

A growing condition of the consumption of images, ideas, and events from which contemporary architecture cannot excuse itself, increasingly interested as it is to keep up with technological development and social demand, at the cost of losing even those few remaining shreds of an identity increasingly open to discussion.

The very concept of 'recent past' can therefore prove to be a temporal and conceptual scale that is useful to an investigation of the complex and heterogeneous realities with which one is dealing and in which contemporary architecture is working, forced continually to participate in an interplay of scales, ranging from the globalization of images and the specificity of context, between the times of the New Economy and the structural slowness of architectural construction.

The succession of complex phenomena linked one to another, the mobility of the characters involved and their culture of origin, the continual mediation and the contrast between common taste, consolidated traditions, and modernization, the rising economic and geographic scale, as well as that of the processes of urbanization demand a degree of analysis of the event that cannot be on a direct basis with the contemporary, nor cannot be consumed in the exemplary nature of microhistory, nor can it seek out only the reasons for what is taking place in a long-term concept that seems to be painted into a corner by the impetuous progress of the various realities.

These are some of the considerations of an exquisitely methodological nature that emerged in taking on an analysis of the last ten years of North American architecture in relation to a political, social, and economic context that is subject to a sweeping metamorphosis.

A decade of changes in which architecture struggled to offer images that properly represented it, if not through an appeal to virtuality capable of responding immediately and not without problematic issues to the repeated demands of reality.

A decade that was born under the axe of economic crisis and which ended in the spotlight of an unprecedented productive and financial expansion, conveyed by the affirmation and spread of the Internet on a world scale; a decade that began in the shadow of the fall of the Berlin Wall and the riots of Los Angeles and that ended with the further globalization of America's political role and a growing awareness of a multiracial society in which in certain states of the Union, for the first time, the Hispanic and Asian communities will be in the majority with respect to the white community.

A decade during which projects that had been conceived and designed in the Eighties were slowly brought to completion, experiencing first the effect of 'S,M,L,XL', then the effect of Bilbao-Gehry, and all the while the results of a globalization of ideas and projects that, as never before, has led so many American architects to work and to obtain a definitive consecration in Europe and Asia and, at

Acknowledgements
*This research project could never have been
completed without the concrete and tireless
support of Marazzi on the one hand and
without continual interaction with the
architect Adalberto Dal Lago, mastermind
of the series and tireless quester after new
realities and ideas in architecture. A sincere
thank-you, then, goes to all those, in the
various American studios, helped me
to obtain materials and by discussing
individual projects: Meg Alpine (Cesar
Pelli), Elisabetta Annovi (Aldo Rossi
Associati), Will Bruder and Dwayne Smith
(William P. Bruder), Lise Ann Couture
and Hani Rashid (Asymptote), Brenna
Dougherty (Rafael Vinoly), Peter Eisenman
and Sebastián (Eisenman Architects), Lisa
Green (Richard Meier), Charles Gwathmey
and Vanessa Ruff (Gwathmey, Siegel),
Ileana La Fontaine (Pei, Cobb, Freed),
Thom Mayne and Anna Moca (Morphosis),
Keith Mendenhall (Frank O. Gehry),
Eric Owen Moss and Raymond (Eric
Owen Moss), Mark Pasnik (Machado and
Silvetti), Michael Rotondi and Marybeth
(Ro.To.), David Shone (Patkau), Billie
Tsien and Vivian Wang (Williams, Tsien),
and Robert Venturi, Sue Scanlon, and
Lauren Jacobi (Venturi, Scott Brown).
A special thank-you goes out to my
American travelling companion and friend
Federico Dal Lago, to Chiara Geracà
for her assistance in preparing this volume
for publication, to Ilaria Mazzoleni,
priceless guide to Los Angeles, to the
Studio Dal Lago and especially to Sabina
Brucoli and Emma Cavazzini, to Laura
Cesari, Pippo Ciorra, Aldo Colonnetti,
Francesco Jodice, Pierluigi Nicolin, Paolo
Scrivano, and Mirko Zardini for their
advice and their encouragement never
to settle for less, and to Marta and Simone
for the warmth with which they have
always been able to surround me.
This book is dedicated to the memory
of Gabriella Bossi.*

the same time, so many Asian and European designers to work in North America.

These years show how the diverse architectural cultures that inhabit the United States are increasingly taking on an awareness of their own role, distant from the traditional centres of academic development and at the same time an image of social and economic realities in expansion.

This volume attempts to open a window on this dimension in flux that is also of great interest by offering a selection of projects built in the Nineties by North American architects in America.

This is an approach that has at least in part been conditioned by the nature of the previous volume belonging to the same series, the *Atlante. Tendenze dell'architettura europea contemporanea. Gli anni Novanta*, edited by Marco De Michelis in 1997. An attempt to make a selection that immediately leads us to take on a theme that has been entirely ignored over recent decades, i.e., whether we can speak of a national American style, with its own language, traditions, and history. Or whether, as I believe, a series of characteristics, even contradictory one with another, should not be derived from the different artistic and intellectual experiences linked to the various economic, social, and geographic contexts (let us not forget that in the final analysis we are after all speaking of a federation of states), thus composing an account that defines at least the uncertain boundaries of American architecture today.

The selection attempts to reflect not only the different conceptual and artistic processes of development, but also the multiplicity of constructive and functional typologies involved.

In our selection we have always attempted to avoid being overshadowed by the clamour for the new thing and the most recent piece of work, rather than trying to identify the most significant creation in the career of a single architect created in the U.S.A. during the Nineties.

These brief essays are entrusted with the task of further extending the gaze with respect to a reality that clearly cannot be condensed into eighteen projects and the experience of eighteen architects.

In their turn, the essays refer the reader to a thematic and critical breakdown that attempts to focus on several of the most evident characteristics in American architecture of the last decade, intersecting them with several of the more macroscopic changes in society and the territory.

The themes involved attempt to compose a problematic fresco that ranges from the metamorphosis underway in the North American continent under the impulse of economic and social growth that continues to counterbalance phenomena of powerful globalization against opposing thrusts of the recovery of regional and local traditions. The first two chapters (*Mutations vs Globalization* and *Critical Regionalism*) therefore attempt to explore the slow and contradictory mutation of American architecture in relation to a traditional clientele that is often timid and conservative, the difficulty of interaction between official culture and the complexity of reality and, too often, the flight into a spectacular vision of the architectural object. While on the other hand it is possible to note the reinforcement of certain regional design experiences that attempt to seek out a mediation between context, its environmental value, and a less invasive modernity.

The task of the third chapter (*Learning from…*) is, instead, that of taking into account a lengthy reflection on the part of American architecture concerning itself and the tools with which it works, generating a number of theoretical and design experiences of particular impact on the contemporary international debate.

Aldo Rossi and America

'America is certainly an important page in the scientific autobiography of my projects, even though I arrived there rather late in my career'
(Aldo Rossi)

Any attempt to reconstruct the complex array of relationships between Aldo Rossi and the U.S.A. would, I believe, be one of the most interesting approaches to understanding, at least in the first phase, that fine red line that connects the avant-garde architectural culture of the East Coast with Venice and its Department of Architecture.

These are still faint traces, confused and too strongly conditioned by the taste for the anecdotal and the autobiographical to lead to significant results, even if, over recent years, and especially after Rossi's tragic death, we have seen the first research projects and interventions capable of offering an interesting grid for an understanding[1] of the phenomenon. The object of this brief essay and this particular section of the book[2] is to recount briefly some of the events that have marked the relationship between Rossi and America, including several significant passages from A *Scientific Autobiography* and the public projects developed between 1986 and 1991. From the first drawings exhibited in New York in the early Seventies to the Thomas Jefferson Medal in Architecture of 1991, we can witness a gradual metamorphosis in the American relationships and friendships of Rossi, increasingly the tireless traveller, increasingly a citizen of the world, capable of universalizing his own memory, his own biographical career of images and figures in every project that he undertook.

Paradoxically, Rossi's success in America developed first of all out of his drawings and the impact that they had on the American architectural culture of the early Seventies, balanced between a rescovery of purist rationalism through the work of the Five and the rude shoves of the postmodern.

The drawings, then, and not the theoretical writings, which only later, and specifically between 1981 and 1982,[3] were translated into English. The drawings that were to be exhibited at the Cooper Union at the behest of John Hejduk and which, at the same time, were to become tools of investigation and debated in

the two writings of Manfredo Tafuri[4] and Rafael Moneo[5] for *Oppositions* issues 3 and 5 in a period straddling the XV Triennale of Milan in 1973 in which Rossi himself undertook a significant representational and epistemological revision of rational architecture.

Dating back to 1976 were the first lectures at the Cooper Union and at Cornell University, followed by a first collaboration with the Institute for Architecture and Urban Studies in New York (IAUS), which led to the 1979 book, *Aldo Rossi in America*.

In the Eighties, Rossi gradually became more and more accepted on the international scene through his built projects, his design objects, and his drawings, which were transformed into a recognized trademark. And the same is true in the United States where there were numerous opportunities for teaching (Yale, 1980; Harvard-GSD, 1983; Walter Gropius Lecture at Harvard, 1989) and the first architectural work with the project for the campus of the University of Miami in 1986, the triumphal arch in Galveston (1987), the lighthouse theatre in Toronto (1988), and the single-family house in the Pocono Mountains in Pennsylvania (1988), all projects always undertaken with the collaboration of Morris Adjmi. In 1990 he received the Pritzker Prize which was tantamount to the definitive consecration of Aldo Rossi; in 1991 he received the AIA Honor Award and the Thomas Jefferson Medal in Architecture, marking a well established bond with American architectural culture.

Dating from the early Nineties are some of the projects for Disney in Orlando and in Paris, but especially the architectural intervention for the South Bronx Academy of Art in New York, in which Rossi joins the appeal of the artist Tim Rollins to intervene in one of the most run-down areas in the city. Dating from the last years were the projects for the office buildings for Walt Disney in Los Angeles and on Broadway in New York (1984), while the following year saw the project for a single-family home in Seaside, near Miami. *(L.M.)*

[1] I am referring especially to: Joan Oackman (edited by), *Architectural Culture 1943-1968*, New York, Columbia/ Rizzoli, 1993; Michael K. Hays (edited by), *Oppositions Reader*, New York, Princeton Architectural Press, 1998.
[2] In the first volume, Marco De Michelis (edited by), *Atlante. Tendenze dell'architettura europea contemporanea. Gli anni Novanta*, homage was paid to the work of Ignazio Gardella.
[3] Aldo Rossi, *The Architecture of the City*, Opposition Books, Cambridge (Mass.), MIT Press, 1982 (translation by Joan Oackman and Diane Ghirardo); Aldo Rossi, *A Scientific Autobiography*, Opposition Books, Cambridge (Mass.), MIT Press, 1981 (translation by Lawrence Venuti)
[4] Manfredo Tafuri, 'L'Architecture dans le Boudoir', in *Oppositions*, no. 3, May 1974.
[5] Rafael Moneo, 'Aldo Rossi: The Idea of Architecture and the Modena Cemetery', in *Oppositions*, no. 5, June 1976.

From 'A Scientific Autobiography'

'America is certainly an important page in the scientific autobiography of my projects, even though I arrived there rather late in my career. Still, time prepares one in strange ways. While my early education was influenced by American culture, this influence occurred mostly through the cinema and literature; for me, American things were never "objects of affection", I am referring particularly to North American culture, since I have always viewed Latin America as a source of fantastic invention, and I used to consider myself, proudly and presumptuously, a Hispanophile.

'Moreover, I could not respond with any first-hand experience to the descriptions, books, and images furnished by the architects of the American city. In fact, even when I was accused of being too immersed in books, especially as a boy, I was always concerned with the relation between study and direct experience. This is perhaps another reason that I have not completely lost my ties with Lombardy, and that I manage to mix, as it were, old sensations with new impressions.

'In any case, I realized at a certain point that the official criticism of architecture had not included America or, what was worse, had not looked at it: the critics were preoccupied only with seeing how modern architecture had been transformed or applied in the United States. This also was connected with a vague anti-fascism, a search for the modern city, and many other beautiful things of which social democratic culture has always sought examples without ever finding them.

'Yet it is well known that in no place has modern architecture failed so badly as in the United States. If there is a transplant or transformation that ought to be studied, it lies in the great Parisian architecture of the Beaux-Arts period, in academic German architecture, and naturally in the most profound aspects of the English city and countryside — not to mention the Spanish Baroque architecture in Latin America, which offers a similar situation.

'I believe that no city better than New York so plainly confirms the truth of the theses I set forth in *The Architecture of the City*. New York is a city of stone and monuments such as I never believed could exist, and on seeing it, I realized how Adolf Loos's project for the *Chicago Tribune* competition was his interpretation of America, and not of course, as one might have thought, a Viennese *divertissement*: it was his synthesis of the distortions created in America by an extensive application of a style in a new context. And the area which surrounds this city-monument is the entire vast territory of the country (…)

'If I were to speak now of my American work or "formation", I would be digressing too far from the scientific autobiography of my projects and would be entering into a personal memoir or a geography of my experience. I will say only that in this country, analogies, allusions, or call them observations, have produced in me a great creative desire and also, once again, a strong interest in architecture.

'For example, I found walking on Sunday mornings through the Wall Street area to be as impressive as walking through a realized perspective by Serlio or some other Renaissance treatise-writer. I have had a similar experience in the villages of New England, where a single building seems to constitute the city or village, independent of its size.

'In 1978, when I was teaching at The Cooper Union, I gave my students the theme of the "American academical village". This theme interested me because it has many references in this culture which are truly foreign to Europeans: for example, the very concept of the "campus". The results of this assignment seemed extraordinary to me, because they rediscovered older themes and went back beyond the unique order of Thomas Jefferson's "academical village" to the architecture of forts, to the New World where the old was silence, above all' (pp. 108–10).

Collaborator: Morris Adjmi

Project for the Campus of the University of Miami, Florida, 1986

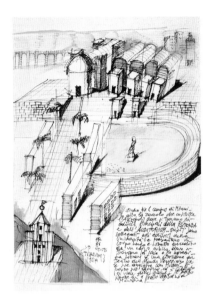

Preparatory studies

General plan

Longitudinal cross-section

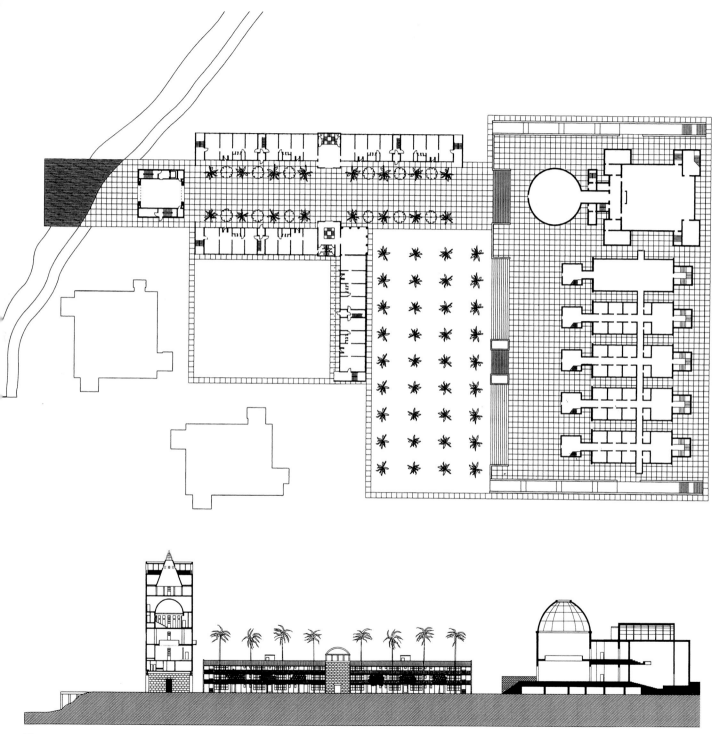

South Bronx Academy of Art,
New York, 1991

Study sketches

General model

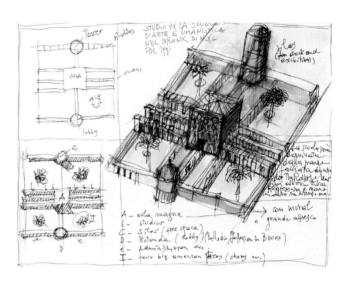

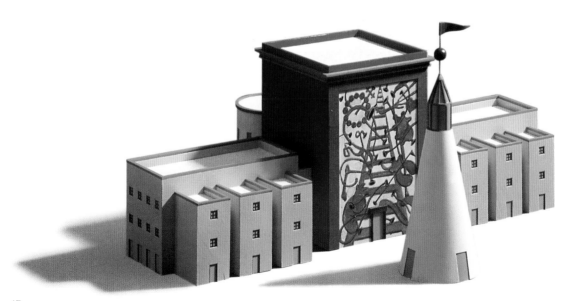

Mutations vs Globalization

The Federal Building
in Oklahoma City
destroyed in 1995

In 1933 King Kong, clutching the glittering new Empire State Building, died under a hail of bullets from attack planes, falling to his death from the skyscraper.

Once the mists of the battle had cleared, the monument of stone, cement, and steel remained intact from the aggression of the beast, embodying the irrational.[1]

Seventy years later, similar attacks would not have the same results.

In the mist that envelops New York and its seven million inhabitants, transforming the city into an archaic and labyrinthine jungle, Godzilla wanders and, in the arc of 137 minutes of film, pulverizes, with the involuntary assistance of the army, not only the Empire State Building, but also the Met (by Gropius/TAC), the Flatiron Building, the Brooklyn Bridge, and Madison Square Garden.

Two years before, the umpteenth extraterrestrial invasion had destroyed, in the days leading up to Independence Day, the White House, the Capitol, and the Statue of Liberty,[2] as well as most of the cities in America.

The recognized icons of America and its modernity crumbled under the attacks of the new invaders, leaving America orphaned of the symbols that represent her today, in a world that has undergone such rapid change.

Mass-market cinema often seems to register the deepest feelings of society, exorcizing them, and it is striking to notice this apparent savagery against the representative symbols of the nation just one year after the terrorist attack on the federal building of Oklahoma City.

In a condition in which the world of official architecture accounts for 10 percent of the space built in the U.S., mirroring and exacerbating a world trend that increasingly indicates a sharp separation between architecture and construction, one begins to wonder whether we can still expect from architecture the capacity to conceive of contemporary spaces with which an entire nation can identify.

A new vigorous economic phase that is mirrored, despite a terrifying national debt,[3] by the growth of the New Economy symbolized by the capricious but powerful development of Nasdaq. The complication of the American social and cultural structure triggered by the contant growth of different ethnic 'minorities'. The definitive affirmation of the Internet as a model of communication and exchange of information and the natural shift toward the globalization of the political and economic role of America, especially after the fall of the Berlin Wall in 1989. These are just a few of the elements that represent a profound change in the North American continent and at the same time trigger the identification of images and icons capable of representing it.[4]

The mechanism that seemed to link phases of economic expansion and civil and political tension to new architectural experimentation seems today apparently suspended between a public and private clientele that rarely has the courage to attempt new paths and which insists on stale and old-fashioned formal and linguistic stereotypes and the official architectural culture, blinded by the star-system, only rarely opposed by a school of criticism that is too concerned with being 'politically correct', happily cloistered in its own world, strongly tied to the university system and reluctant to deal with such complex issues.

With the disappearance over at least the past thirty years of a political demand capable of summoning architecture to make itself the standard-bearer of new social messages,[5] the progressive destiny of American architecture seems to have been entrusted over this past decade primarily to university institutions, recipients in recent years of major federal investments and constantly in competition one with another against the major museums, in which the traditional competition among the great tycoons of culture such as the Guggenheim, MoMA, and the Getty have been joined by other public and private institutions distributed along the national territory and with a few enlightened economic subjects.

An elite dimension of demand that

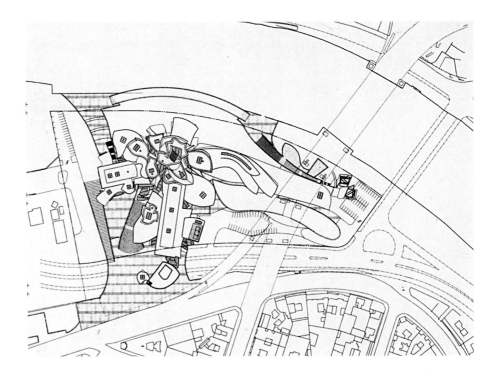

translates into a supply that is often timid or excessively conditioned by a need to spectacularize the architectural object to make it accessible to mass consumption.[6]

While it appears significant that, especially beginning in the second half of the Eighties, the success of several of the more interesting protagonists of contemporary American architecture has been achieved outside of their own country in a curious interplay that also brought European and Asian designers to work on new public works in the United States.

A success that was in part heralded by the progressive cultural influence that certain American universities began to have, especially in Asia and South America, and which on the other hand saw the reinforcement of the traditional tie with Europe, exemplified perfectly by the recent history, first of *Oppositions*[7] and later of *ANY*.

The MoCA by Arata Isozaki, the De Menill Collection in Houston by Renzo Piano, the expansion of Columbia University by Bernard Tschumi, the new Museum of Modern Art by Rafael Moneo in Houston, the projects for Los Angeles by Rem Koolhaas, the Museum of Modern Art of San Francisco by Mario Botta,

the expansion of the Museum of Modern Art of Milwaukee by Santiago Calatrava, and the various American projects by Aldo Rossi, along with the constant presence of these same personalities in the most important American universities, showed a historic phase of exchanges and powerful influences from overseas.

But the same could be said of the designs and works built by Frank Gehry,[8] Peter Eisenman,[9] Richard Meier,[10] Robert Venturi,[11] Steven Holl,[12] I.M. Pei, Rafael Vinoly, Cesar Pelli,[13] Helmut Jahn, and Michael Graves.

Interventions that develop in different manners, which range from the design of typologically and culturally 'American' buildings in contexts involving major financial investments (one good example is the Petronas Twin Towers in Kuala Lumpur by Cesar Pelli; another is the Bank of China by I.M. Pei in Hong Kong, but we should not ignore all the work done by Disney in France), and affirmation through international competitions (this is the case of the Sainsbury Wing in London by Venturi and Scott Brown or the new Museum of Contemporary Art in Helsinki by Steven Holl), all the way out to experimentation in extreme design projects capable of becoming in

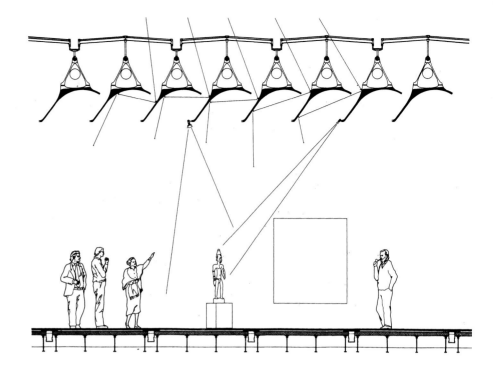

Michael Graves, Team
Disney Building, Burbank,
California, 1985–91

a second phase models that can exported due to the powerful impact on international public opinion (from the pyramids by Pei for the Louvre to the Guggenheim of Bilbao by Frank Gehry replicatted in design for the second, new building in New York).

In any case, in all of these cases, the project was seen above all as an investment in the quality and originality of image capable of being transformed into a powerful marketing tool for the company or institution that promoted it. From this point of view, we should consider symptomatic the success enjoyed by Frank Gehry's work, especially after the inauguration of the Guggenheim in Bilbao. Precisely the case of the Guggenheim in New York becomes symbolic to any understanding of the complex relationship between client and contemporary monument in America.

On the one hand, the restoration and expansion of F.L. Wright's Guggenheim by Gwathmey and Siegel brought to light a delightful paradox in which the attacks on the expansion, which was in fact timid and respectful of the original design, echoed the very same attacks that had been made thirty years previous upon the inauguration of Wright's creation, while at the same time underscoring the problem of conserving the monuments of modern American architecture.

On the other hand, the recent project for the second site of the Guggenheim by Gehry clearly shows that the client preferred to experiment in a dimension distant from the American continent and then to bring home a model that had been recognized collectively and commercially.

This timidity seems to be mirrored in a generalized conservative dimension represented both by the economic and academic elites, forgetful of that concept of utopia that nourished for over a century the American dream and the research into the relationship between built form and advanced new technologies pursued from Sullivan to Buckminster Fuller and the Eameses.

The narcosis triggered by over-nourishment of images[14] may on the one hand have provoked a tendency that is careful primarily about the spectacular and commercial impact of architecture in which, among the projects for Disney by Michael Graves, the malls by John Jarde, and the recent projects by Gehry, there exists no substantial difference save in terms of

Richard Meier, Exhibition
and Assembly Building,
Ulm, Germany, 1986–93

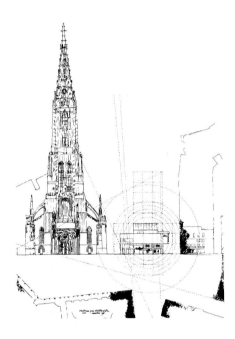

the language employed, while, on the other hand, it seems to have paradoxically reinforced that modernist inertia that nourished so much good American professionalism, from I.M. Pei to Cesar Pelli passing by way of Rafael Vinoly and Richard Meier.

An architecture of great quality and solidity, easily applied and exported, in keeping with an open-minded and prudent client, but unable to dream for the collective and to call on innovative typologies and forms that are not consumed in a simple and passing fashion.

At this point, we seem to be confronted once again by the age-old question concerning the difficulty of identifying in our times a contemporary value of monumentality that is recognized by all communities and their symbolic and spatial qualities.

Will the Getty Center by Richard Meier, or the new Catholic cathedral by Rafael Moneo paired with the Walt Disney Concert Hall by Frank Gehry in Los Angeles be recognized as collective monuments? Or are the real monuments the large infrastructural works, the information superhighways, the new urban parks such as the little Robert F. Wagner Jr Park in New York by Machado and Silvetti, the malls, the theme parks, or the anonymous residential sprawl that surrounds the large metropolises?

The dematerialized surfaces of so much minimalist architecture, the organic skins with which Frank Gehry wraps his most recent works, the cloud of steam in which Diller+Scofidio wanted to float architecture over the lake of

Neûchatel, the flight toward the virtualization of public space through the web seem to indicate a headlong and dangerous flight toward an exclusive Arcadia that tends to individualize feeling rather than sharing them, to cause architecture and its uncomfortable gravity to vanish rather than bringing it back into discussion in order to give life to new spaces for meeting and useful silence.[15]

[1] *King Kong*, directed by Merian C. Cooper and Ernest B. Schoedsack, 102', USA 1933.
[2] I am referring to: *Independence Day*, directed by Roland Emmerich (145', USA 1996) and *Godzilla* by the same producers, and also directed by Emmerich (137', USA 1998).
[3] *Federal Debt*, in Richard Saul Wurman (edited by), *Understanding USA*, Tedx, R. R. Donnelley & Sons, 2000.
[4] 'There can be no doubt that architecture is used in the United States as a culture of representation. (...) For all these reasons special emphasis is placed on the image of architecture that recomposes and organizes or the architecture that shifts elements of disquiet onto the aesthetic plane, or decomposes contrasts, or reconciles them in the memory of the past', Vittorio Gregotti, 'USA, un paese diverso', in *Casabella*, no. 586–587, January-February 1992, p. 5.
[5] Concerning the relationship between politics, architecture, and civil issues in the United States following the Second World War, see: Alexander Tzonis, Liane Lefaivre, Richard Diamond, *Architecture in North America since 1960*, London, Thames and Hudson, 1995, and Liane Lefaivre, Alexander Tzonis, *Planning and Tomatoes*, Casabella, no. 586–587, January-February 1992, pp. 46–49.
[6] '(...) the role that architecture is often called upon to performer is that of smoke and mirrors. The avant-garde architects of today (...) have the task of preparing the ground for the future marketing and transformation of working-class neighbourhoods into luxury developments', Joan Oackman, Nicholas Adams, 'Forme dello spettacolo', in *Casabella*, no. 673-674, December 1999-January 2000, p. 4.

Rafael Moneo, Museum
of Fine Arts, Houston,
1992–2000

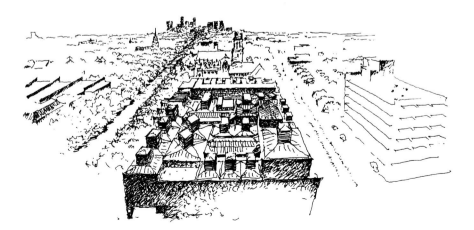

Peter Eisenman, Max
Reinhardt Haus, Berlin,
1992

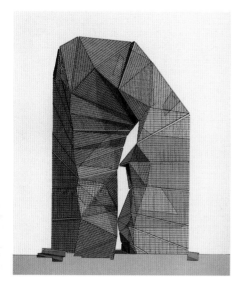

[7] Michael K. Hays (edited by), *Oppositions Reader*, New York, Princeton Architectural Press, 1998.

[8] Among the most significant creations by Frank Gehry outside of the U.S., we should mention: The Vitra Museum in Weil am Rhein, Germany, 1987–89, and the Vitra Offices in Birsfelden, Basel, 1988–94; the American Center, Paris, 1988–93; the Entertainment Center at EuroDisney, Marnela-Vallée, Paris, 1989–92; the Guggenheim Museum, Bilbao, 1991–97; Building of the Nationale-Nederlanden, Prague, 1994–96; Der neue Zollhof, Düsseldorf, 1994–99; DG Bank, Berlin, 1995–99; Porta di Venezia, Venice, 1998.

[9] Among the most significant creations by Peter Eisenman built in Europe and Japan, we should mention: design for a Piazza Cannaregio, Venice, 1978; Iba Checkpoint Charlie Residence, Berlin, 1981–85; Biocentrum, design, Frankfurt am Main, 1986–87; Koizumi Sangyo Office Building, Tokyo, 1988–90; Nunotani Headquarters, Tokyo, 1990–92; Max Reinhardt House, design, Berlin, 1992; BFL Software, Bangalore, India, 1996; Monument to the Victims of the Holocaust, Berlin, 1998–2001.

[10] Among the most significant European creations by Richard Meier we should mention: Building for conferences and exhibitions, Ulm, 1986–93; Town Hall and Central Library, The Hague, 1986–95; Royal Dutch Paper Mills, Hilversum, Holland, 1987–92; Museum of Contemporary Art, Barcelona, 1987–95; Canal Plus, general headquarters, Paris, 1988–92; Hypolux Bank, Luxembourg, 1989–93; Daimler Benz Research Center, Ulm, 1989–92; Euregio Offices, Basel, 1990–98; Hans Arp Museum, Rolandseck, Germany, 1991–2000; Church of the Year 2000, Rome, 1996–2001.

[11] Among the most significant creations by Venturi and Scott Brown outside the U.S.A. we should mention: Sainsbury Wing, National Gallery, London, 1986–91; expansion of the Stedelijk Museum, design, Amsterdam, 1992; Hotel du Département de la Haute-Garonne, Toulouse, 1992–99; Hotel Mielparque Resort Complex, Nikko, Kirifuri, Japan, 1992–97.

[12] For the work done outside of America by Steven Holl we should mention: Makuhari Residences, Chiba, Japan, 1992–97; Nexus World, Fukuoka, Japan, 1989–91; Museum of Contemporary Art, Helsinki, 1993–98; pavilion, Amsterdam, 1998–2000.

[13] The reputation outside of the U.S.A. of Cesar Pelli, I.M. Pei, and Rafael Vinoly is linked primarily to three major urban projects that received enormous attention in the international press: Pei for his expansion and design of the general renovation of the Louvre in Paris; Cesar Pelli for the Petronas Twin Towers in Kuala Lumpur, currently the tallest towers on earth; and Rafael Vinoly for the Opera House in Tokyo.

[14] Concerning this concept, one should read two essays, the first with a generally positive vision on the relationship with excess images, Robert Venturi, *Iconography and Electronics upon a Generic Architecture*, Cambridge (Mass.), MIT Press, 1996, and the second with a sharply more cynical view, Neil Leach, *The Anaesthetics of Architecture*, Cambridge (Mass.), MIT Press, 1999.

[15] 'Perhaps that is all that architecture will succeed in achieving in the century to come. Perhaps the slow spaces will have to become spaces in which one escapes from utility, from value, and from all the other contributing factors that make buildings visible. In other words, perhaps architecture will only be able to exist in the construction of these times of self-reflection that still have moments of meaning for our society', in Aaron Betsky, 'Computer blobs, wood shacks and slow space', in *Domus*, no. 816, June 1999, p. 29.

Cesar Pelli, Petronas Twin
Towers, Kuala Lumpur,
Malaysia, 1991–97

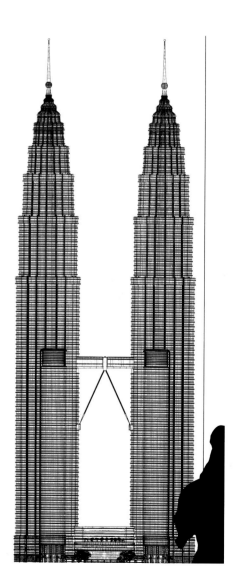

Addition to the Solomon R. Guggenheim Museum, New York, 1982–92

Gwathmey, Siegel & Associates Architects
Project architect: J. Alspector
Structures: Severud-Szegedy

The expansion of the Solomon R. Guggenheim Museum could be viewed as the first true public debate to arise in the United States from the restoration and modification of an icon of North American architectural culture.

A paradoxical twist of fate if we think of the violent criticism leveled at F.L. Wright when the museum opened in 1959.

The original building, which comprised two circular structural bodies linked by a horizontal connection, had already undergone a first, major intervention between 1963 and 1968 under the supervision of the Taliesin studio, with the construction of a four-storey building behind it, as previously planned by Wright.

The dizzying growth of the museum collection of modern art and the acquisition of the important Thannauser Collection had required an expansion of the exhibition spaces available, at the expense of administrative offices.

Between the Seventies and the Eighties, the museum enjoyed a growing popularity stimulated by a new cultural and promotional policy on the part of the Guggenheim's Board, built primarily under the direction of Thomas Krens beginning from the early Eighties, transforming Wright's Guggenheim into the beating heart of the most important cultural 'multinational' on a global scale.

The serious material conditions of the building (the materials used were cheap, and they led to numerous problems with dampness, while the skylight and casements had no thermal insulation) and the need of finally putting some order in the way the various collections housed in the museum were exhibited, led to a commission for the studio Gwathmey, Siegel & Associates Architects in 1982 for a task of restoring and expanding the museum, which continued until 1992.

And this second intervention likewise continued along the outlines of the Wright model, based as it was on the expansion done in the Sixties, whose foundations were engineered to support the weight of a ten-storey building.

The overall plan, then, called for a doubling of the gallery space, an expansion of the storage area, relocating the library and the archives, as well as increasing the area of the bookstore and restaurant, all the while devoting complete care to the original plans of Wright himself, and often reutilizing the original furnishings and materials.

The new tower grafted with ease into the system of the two circular structures, with which it attempted to compose a new exhibition unit, while on the exterior it seems that the determination not to disturb the majestic mass of Wright's museum prevailed over all other design decisions.

The Guggenheim Museum and its expansion in relation to existing buildings and Central Park

The expansion seen on 89th Street

Solution proposed
by Frank Lloyd Wright

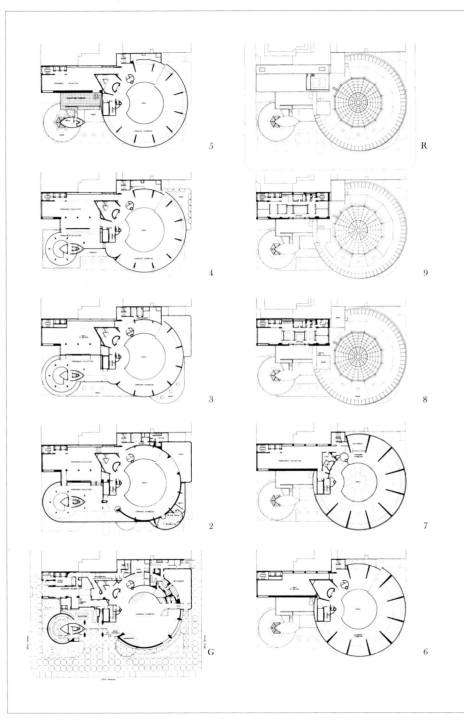

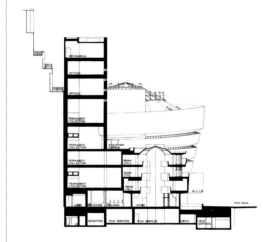

Plans, from the ground
floor G to the roofs R

Transverse cross-section
of the new rooms for
the permanent exhibition

Interior passageway
between the small
Rotunda and the new
exhibition spaces

Detail of the façade
on 89th Street

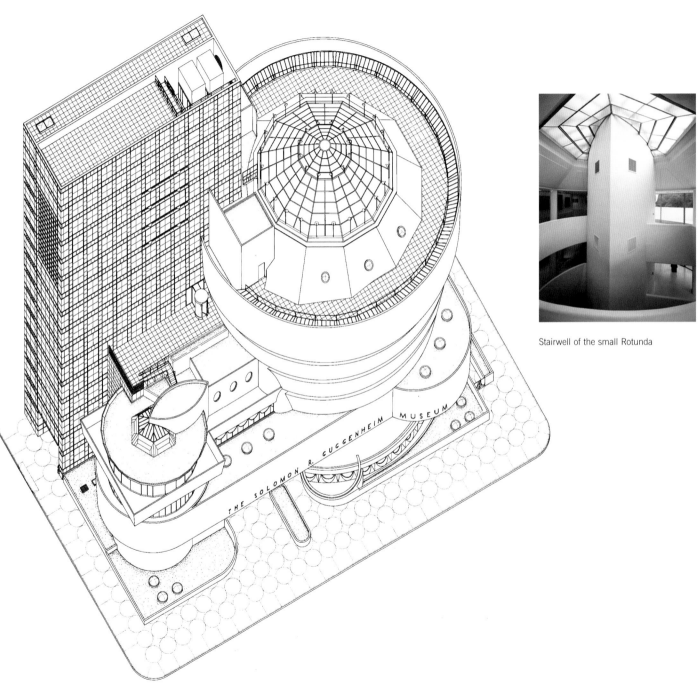

Stairwell of the small Rotunda

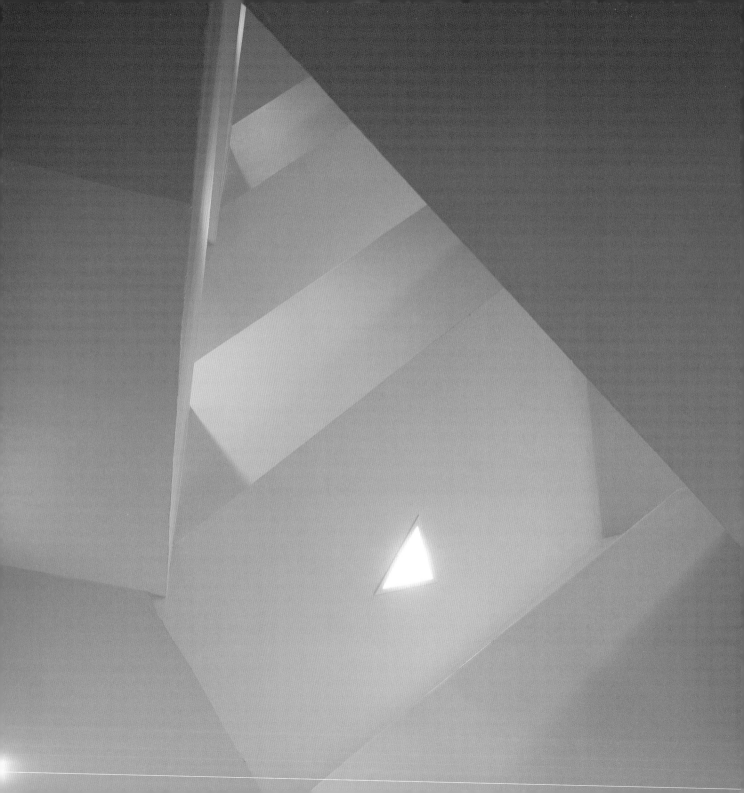

Interior of the stairwell

The new hall for the
permanent collections

The new exhibition
spaces in relationship
to the existing spaces

The new entry ramp

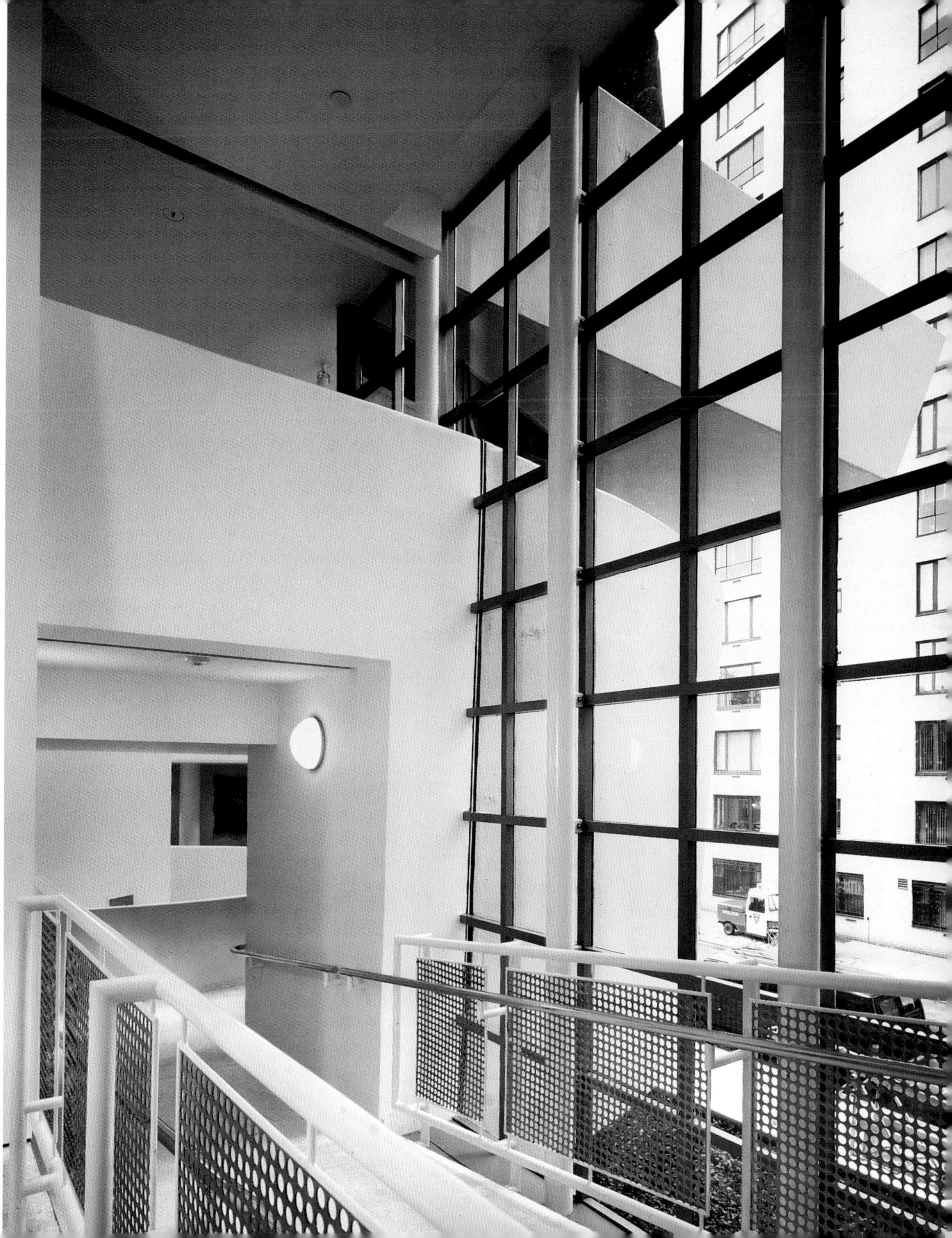

Getty Center, Los Angeles, California, 1984–97

Richard Meier and Associates
Richard Meier with D.E. Barker, M. Palladino
Landscape design: Emmet L. Wemple & Associates

The J. Paul Getty
Museum, seen from
the central garden

The Getty Research
Institute for the History
of Art and Humanities

'In my mind's eye I see a classic structure, elegant and timeless, emerging serene and ideal, from rough hillside, a kind of Aristotelian structure within the landscape.'

The vision described by Richard Meier in 1984 after one of his first visits to the hills being Santa Monica, where the new Getty Center would in time be built, perfectly delineates the spirit and the very essence of the project.

A new acropolis for the arts in the most anticlassical and unstable city in America; a visible sign in the immense panorama of this metropolis, suspended among the hill, white with travertine and steel.

The museum and research complex is built on an area of 110 acres and underwent a long design and administrative process that led, after fourteen years, to the definitive inauguration and public opening.

Strict building codes that limited the height and size of the buildings, along with a topographic structure marked by a fork in two hilly ridges in the southern sector, overlooking Los Angeles, have sharply conditioned the design of the complex.

The general organization calls for the visitor to reach the Getty Center only via a monorail shuttle that leaves from the valley below, connected directly to the San Diego Freeway and equipped with underground parking facilities.

The process of reaching the centre is designed to reveal progressively the complexity of the Getty Center and the majestic view of Los Angeles that can be enjoyed from the terraces and gardens. By car, one approaches rapidly, passing under the shadow of the Getty as if it were an ancient bastion set to defend the acropolis, then one is swallowed up in the parking garages, and one follows the flow of visitor channeled into the 'propylaea' from here a little shuttle train takes one slowly to the very shoulders of the complex, in an arrival plaza which allows the visitor to take in at a glance the auditorium, the entrance to the museum area, the information centre, and, in the distance, the research institute. Along a natural line that leads from the arrival through the museum courtyard all the up to a great set of terraces suspended over Los Angeles, one perceives the effort of the designer to mediate between geometric structure of the complex and the topography, continually referring the view of the new architecture to the surrounding landscape.

The entire complex is based on a necessary separation of the areas intended for the public at large, such as the museum, the auditorium, the gardens, and the various restaurants, and those buildings used by the researchers and conservators of the several collections of the Getty.

The visitor may in fact move freely along the system of terraces, gardens, and open spaces that mediate among the various buildings, or else enter the large lobby that distributes to the two levels of the museum, organized according to chronological sequence and in keeping with the conservation of the materials and organized with the picture gallery on the upper floor, illuminated by natural light, and the photographic collections, the collections of applied arts, and the sculpture collections on the ground floor and on the basement floor.

The heart of the research facilities, on the other hand, is the Getty Research Institute for the History of Art and Humanities, a structure set on the second ridge, slightly isolated from the rest of the complex and with an introverted structure that revolves around the great central library, endowed with more than a million volumes. The choice of materials reinforces the system of hierarchic relationships among the buildings, with the museum and several of the main structures clad in hewn travertine, alternating with the stucco of the interiors and the steel-panel facing of the service areas.

Context

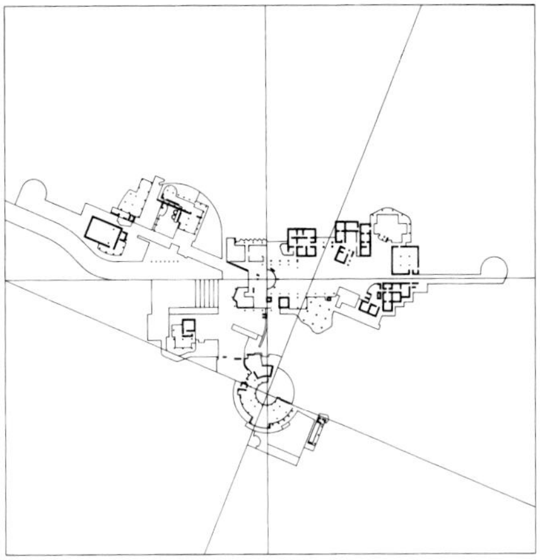

Structure

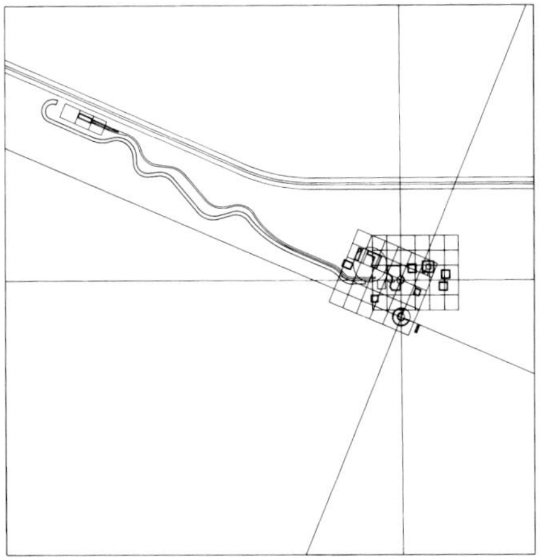

Geometry

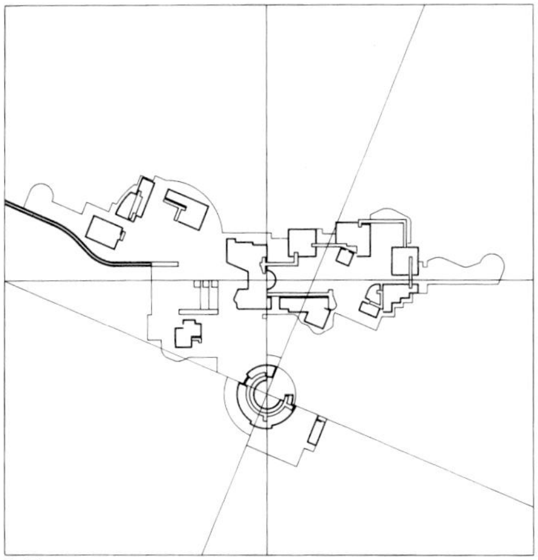

Circulation

Landscape

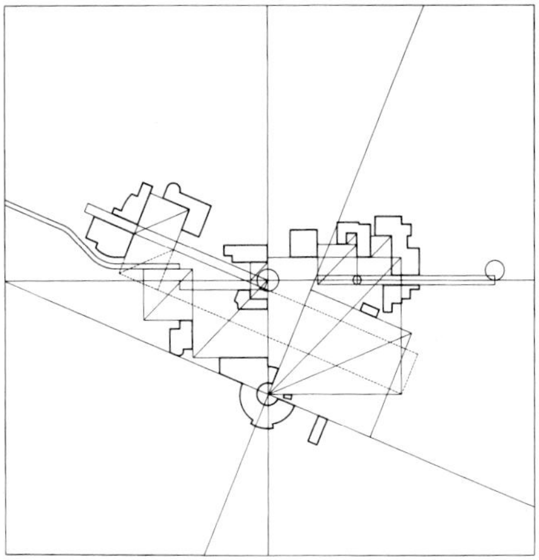

Exterior Spaces

The Getty Foundation
in relation to the city
and the territory

General layout,
general use

Study sketch
of the general layout

Volumetric plan
of the general layout

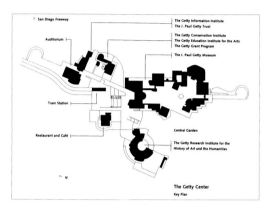

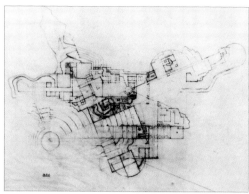

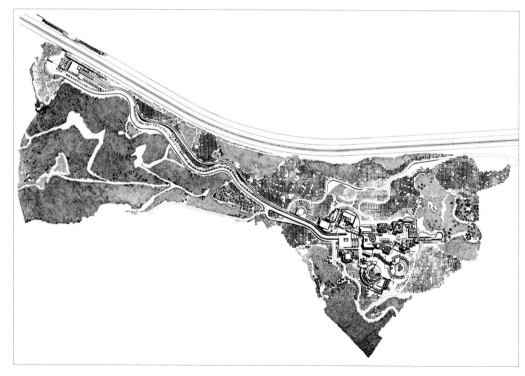

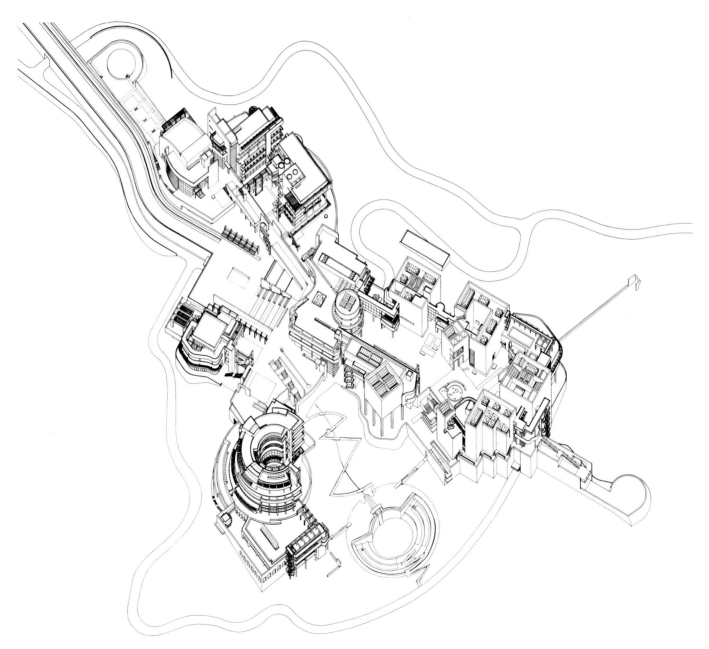

The Auditorium
and the Getty
Conservation Institute,
seen from the restaurant

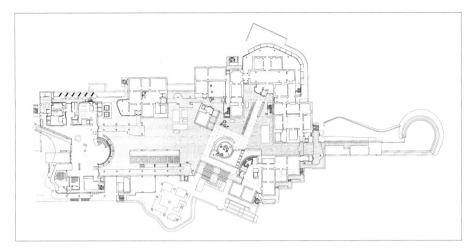

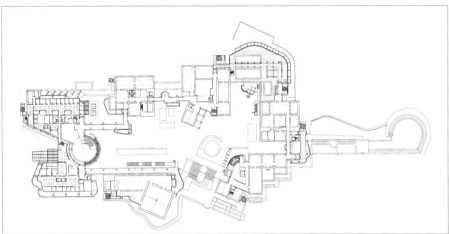

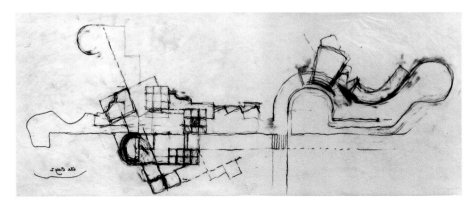

Plan of the entry level

Plan of the upper level

Study sketch

Interior of the library
of the Getty Research
Institute for the History
of Art and Humanities

The central atrium
of the museum

South entrance to
the central courtyard
of the museum

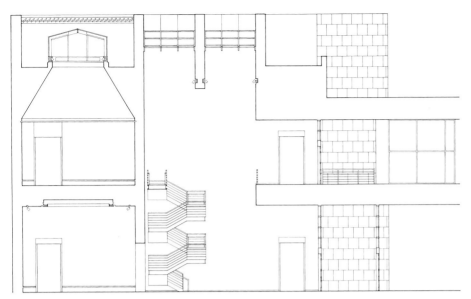

Cross-section of
the exhibition spaces

Hallway leading
to the museum

The Rock and Roll Hall of Fame and Museum, Cleveland, Ohio, 1987–95

Pei, Cobb, Freed & Partners
I.M. Pei with L. Jaebson, M. Flynn, R. Diamond,
J. Sage, W. Kosior, R.P. Madison

A veritable explosion of elementary forms assembled with one another and deformed so as to embody the sweeping power of rock & roll compos the monumental Rock and Roll Hall of Fame and Museum, built as a major entertainment centre and at the same time as a new civic pole capable of revitalizing this outlying area of Cleveland overlooking Lake Erie.

The volumes are put 'in register' by the intersection of the reinforced concrete tower standing more than 50 metres tall, containing the main services and elevators, and the large glassed-in triangular roof, inclined at 45 degrees, which serves as an entrance lobby and, at the same time, as a tent to protect the various exhibition spaces from which the visitors enter and exit to overlook, each time, the majestic central space.

Museum, exhibition, and entertainment functions mix and mingle in a path that alternates spaces closed to the exterior, acoustically and visually in-

sulated, in which one can enjoy in ideal condition the quality of the music 'on display', the theatre equipped with a screen that allows 360 degree projections, and the larger exhibition space located in the basement floor, beneath the level of the lake.

The final destination of this path is the Hall of Fame, a sanctum sanctorum located at the tip of the tower, and containing many of the most important pieces of the collections on display.

The capacity to organize elementary geometric forms, to transform them into elements of urban order as was previously demonstrated in the more important project of the new Louvre in Paris, makes it possible to give meaning to this mass of 14,000 square metres launched on the shores of Lake Erie without falling victim to the temptation of the Hollywood *pastiche* which customarily populates the imaginary world linked to these containers that are hybrids of entertainment and culture.

The entry square
to the museum

The museum in relation
to the lake

The museum in relation
to the city

Ramps leading to the
museum from the street

Basement

Second floor

1 Harbor Promenade
2 Harbor Promenade Entrance
3 Coat Check
4 Ticketing
5 Ahmet M. Ertegun Exhibition
   Hall / Roll Over Beethoven
6 Escalator up to Level 2 Exhibits
7 Restrooms
8 Telephones
9 Museum Offices and Archives

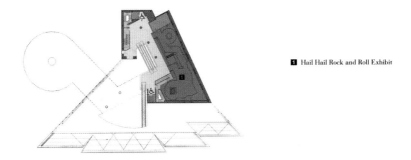

1 Hail Hail Rock and Roll Exhibit

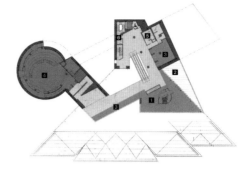

1 Cafe

2 Outdoor Cafe Seating

3 Additional Cafe Seating

4 Level 3 Exhibit and Ramp to L

5 Restrooms

6 Telephones

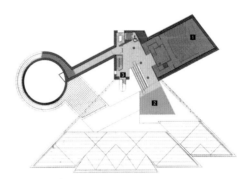

1 It's Only Rock and Roll Cinema

2 Exhibit

3 Stair up to Hall of Fame Lobby

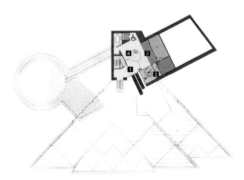

1 Hall of Fame Lobby

2 DJ Booth

3 Induction Ceremonies Exhib

4 Stair up to Hall of Fame

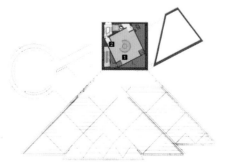

1 Hall of Fame

2 Stair down

Interior of the hall   Transverse cross-section

Main hall

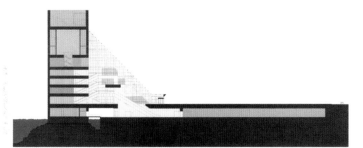

NationsBank Corporate Center, Charlotte, North Carolina, 1987–92

Cesar Pelli & Associates
Cesar Pelli with F. Clarke, T. Duda
Structures: Walter P. Moore & Associates

Volumetric plan
of the general layout

Founder's Hall seen
from the street

Overall view
of NationsBank

Located in the historic and financial heart of Charlotte, the NationsBank Corporate Center may be considered one of the intermediate projects of Cesar Pelli in the path that leads from the great complex of the World Financial Center in New York to the twin towers of Kuala Lumpur in Malaysia.

A design for a 'traditional' skyscraper in the structure, language, and organization that combines the great sixty-storey tower destined prevalently for use as the headquarters of NationsBank, linked to a system of large covered public spaces on the ground floor, representing one of the interesting innovations in the American urban skyscraper of the Eighties and early Nineties.

The base of the tower, standing 875 feet tall, is faced in light beige granite, whose tones tend progressively to lighten to leave space to the glass and anodyzed aluminum facing that leads to a dematerialization in the final part of the tower, inverting the process utilized in New York where the dark granite roofs tended on the other hand

to mark the different heights and geometries of the towers.

Aggregated on the ground floor of the skyscraper is the Founder's Hall, a large public space designed to stimulate the revitalization of the artistic and commercial activities of Charlotte, directly linked to the nearby North Carolina Blumenthal Performing Arts Center, a building meant primarily for entertainment and health.

Founder's Hall, designed as a single large space covered by a glassed-in barrel vault, presents itself at once as an entry hall for the employees of NationsBank and as a place of public performances; moreover, its axial position with respect to the tower and various aggregated structures transforms it into a principal element of union and distribution of the entire complex.

Connected to Founder's Hall is the Overstreet Mall, a sector raised above the urban level, dedicate to commercial activities, linked by several raised passages to the spaces outside the complex.

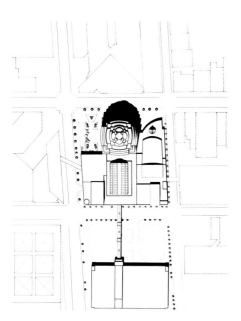

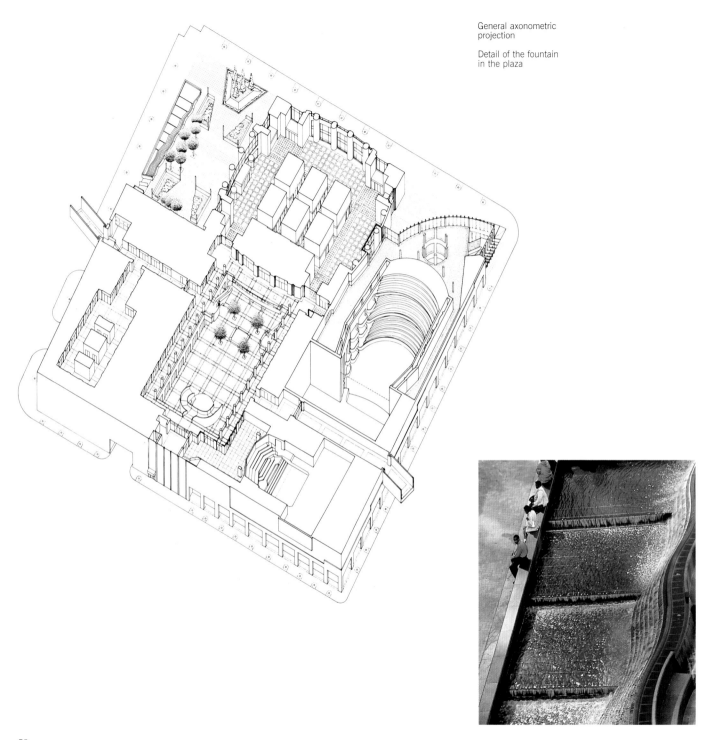

General axonometric
projection

Detail of the fountain
in the plaza

General view

Detail of the head
of the tower

The Performing Arts
Center

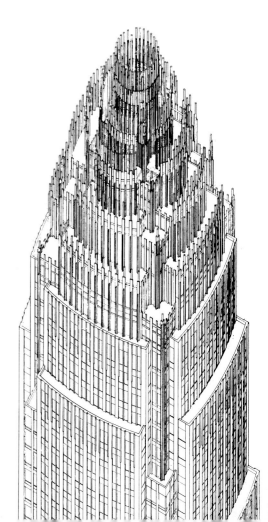

Transverse cross-section
of the atrium

Front of the Founder's
Hall

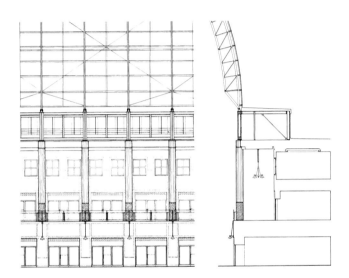

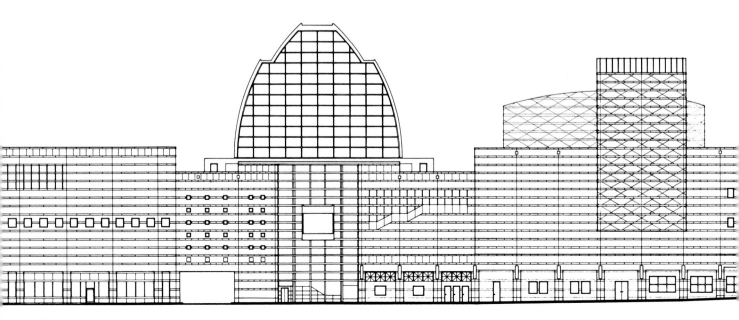

The NationsBank
Corporate Center and
the Performing Arts Center

Founder's Hall seen
from the main atrium

The auditorium   Interior of the first level
of the tower

Elevator block

Palmer Stadium, Princeton, New Jersey, 1998

Rafael Vinoly Architects
Rafael Vinoly with Chan-Li-Lin
Structures: Thorton Tomasetti Eng.
with Structural Design Group

The new stadium of the university campus at Princeton seems to confirm the premise for which it was created: to be considered the most important university stadium in the country and to be a worthy heir to the old Palmer Stadium, built at the turn of the twentieth century, with a capacity of 45,000 spectators.

Built on the same area which once held the first stadium, this new collective monument dedicated to sports strikes an imposing stance with the classical conception of its structure as well as with the very intelligent use of the general sections which allow a continual flow of visitors as well as a level of permeability with the surrounding landscape.

The sports facility is located at the edge of the campus, practically fronting Lake Carnegie along with other structures dedicated to physical activity and leisure time.

Like a great Hellenistic hippodrome, the building establishes itself on the exterior with monumental apertures that evoke the entrance and which allow an intermediate overlook for the stadium, surveying the basin of the playing field and the lower bleachers.

The project fits into a general plan for the reorganization of the Princeton university campus (an area of 300 hectares, along with another 200 hectares of university-owned land) conducted by the studio of Silvetti and Machado from the end of the Eighties to the present day, in which such prestigious designers as Vinoly and Robert Venturi have worked to redefine, with new collective buildings, the edges of the campus in relation to the continually developing urban centre.

With a practice of direct participation in the development of the characteristics of the project, deeply rooted in American universities over the past several decades, studio Vinoly carried on consultations concerning the structure and organization of the stadium that led to the definitive solution in which it was decided to separate the track and field facilities from the playing field, making use of the surface covered by the previous structure to create two new juxtaposed sports facilities.

The stadium is considered one of the most powerful and easily recognized symbols in a complex and heterogeneous university community and the result seems equally to balance the traditional image proper to architecture of the campuses of the East Coast with a design influenced by strongly contemporary technological and structural contents.

The sports complex is organized in two distinct and closely related structures: the first enclosure, with a capacity of 30,000 spectators, dedicated to football and soccer, and a second enclosure, with a much smaller capacity, organized for track and field competition. The stadium is structured like a hippodrome, with its short side used to house the tensostructure roof that protects the bleachers of the track and field stadium, set perpendicular to the other stadium.

On the exterior, the stadium presents itself as a structure composed of prefabricated load-bearing panels made of concrete, clad in a sand-blasting mixture, punctuated by a continuous series of large and distinctly vertical apertures that lead the spectators to a series of terraces that overlook the playing field as well as to a road that runs around the entire perimeter of the stadium, running directly beneath the upper bleachers.

The system of seating is organized into two levels divided in accordance with the elevation of the surrounding campus, while the upper bleachers are of particular interest, fixed with a light system of steel pillars and bridges to the perimeter structure, organized with an intermediate level that channels the spectators to the upper levels and at the same time maintains a continual visual relation with the surrounding park.

The covered pedestrian walkway and the raised connections

At pages 68–69:
The stadium and
the surrounding park

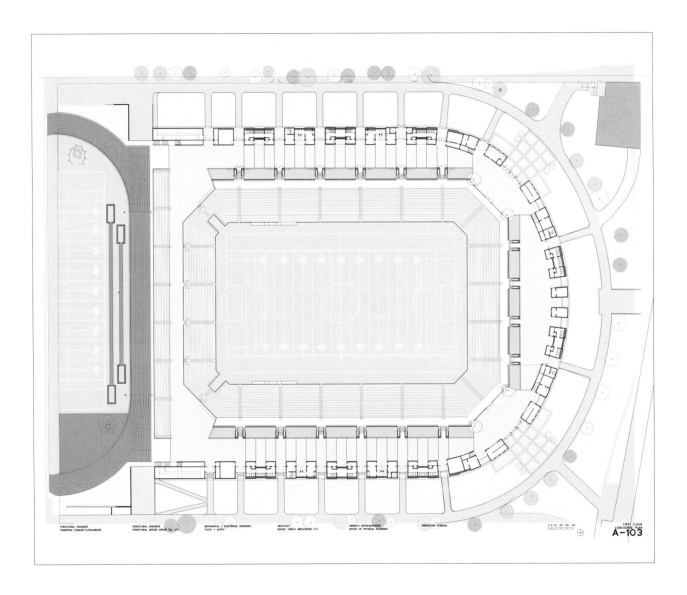

STRUCTURAL ENGINEER
THORNTON TOMASETTI/ENGINEERS

STRUCTURAL ENGINEER
STRUCTURAL DESIGN GROUP CO., LTD.

MECHANICAL / ELECTRICAL ENGINEER
FLACK + KURTZ

ARCHITECT
RAFAEL VIÑOLY ARCHITECTS, P.C.

OWNER'S REPRESENTATIVE
OFFICE OF PHYSICAL PLANNING

PRINCETON STADIUM

FIRST FLOOR
CONCOURSE PLAN
A-103

General location

Study sketch.
Overall view

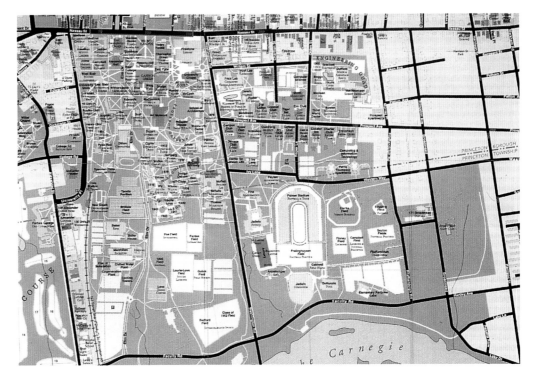

Side front

Longitudinal cross-section

Study sketch.
The relationship between
the two playing fields

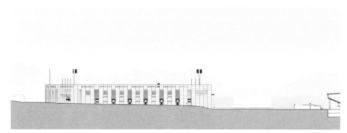 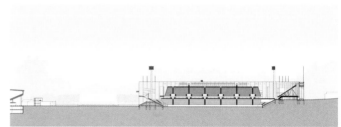

Main entrance
to the stadium

The stadium and the track
and field facilities

The roof of the track
and field bleachers

Connections between
the bleachers and
the interior passageway
to the stadium

The raised bleachers
and the passageways
for the public

Cross-section
of the bleachers

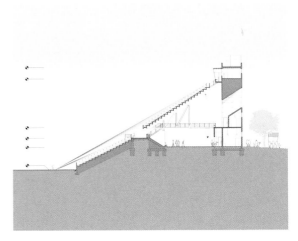

Robert F. Wagner Jr Park, Battery Park City, New York, 1992–96

Machado and Silvetti & Associates
Collaborators: P. Lofgren, D. Dolezal, E. Gibb, N. Tehrani
Landscape design: The Olin Partners
Garden design: Lynden P. Muller Garden Design

Built slowly on account of the economic crisis during the early Nineties, Battery Park has become for New York and especially for Manhattan the most considerable alternative to Central Park in terms of the dimensions involved and the variety of public spaces created.

One of the most important matrices in this sequence of open spaces along the Hudson River is surely represented by Robert F. Wagner Jr Park, located at the foot of downtown, set between the little Museum of the Holocaust by Roche & Dinkerloo and the Battery.

This 3.6 acre space, exceptional in both location and its wealth of environmental references, presents itself with a dual identity as both park and waterfront, and based on this dual identity organizes its general structure and the individual architectural interventions.

The project is based on three components: a pair of pedestrian walkways that lead to the main entrance to the park, joining up with the routes that arrive from Battery Park and Battery Place, two pavilions linked by a bridge that constitute the centre of the park and house the service facilities and a café, as well as a large grassy terrace bounded by a continuous line of benches.

It's a Y-shaped structure that constitutes the spinal cord of the park and at the same a privileged focal point overlooking the Statue of Liberty, a veritable territorial point of focus for this limited architectural intervention.

Beginning with the very first stages of design which not only involved the studio of Machado and Silvetti, but also the landscape designers Hanna/Olin and the garden designer Lynden P. Muller, and which above all witnessed a fierce debate involving all the various elements of society involved, it immediately became evident that the park would have to be organized along a privileged visual relationship with the perception of the Statue of Liberty in one direction and the port of New York in the other.

And the only building designed for the park is organized to accommodate those who stroll along the river, offering them a privileged vista of these civic and American icons.

The structure was conceived as an imposing ruin in brick, carved through the middle by a chasm bridged by a deck on the upper floor.

This 'archaeological remains' was designed to 'withstand' the great architectural mass of downtown, which presses with its twin towers and especially with its massive skyscrapers in brick and stone dating from the turn of the twentieth century, overlooking the Hudson River.

An anomalous object, a wedge that bends slightly just next to the deck which distributes to the two terraces set on the upper floor at a height of five metres, reachable via the two stairways behind. The two terraces, each equipped with a long tall wooden seat, a veritable throne upon which to relax, overlook different horizons: the first is dominated by a large arch which frames the view to the south toward Ellis Island, while the second is open to the north and Governor's Island. From the deck at the centre, along the centre of gravity that delicately governs the entire park, there opens up a vista of the Statue of Liberty.

Detail of the bench
of the terraced meadow

At pages 78–79:
View from the ocean
of the pavilions and
the terraced meadow

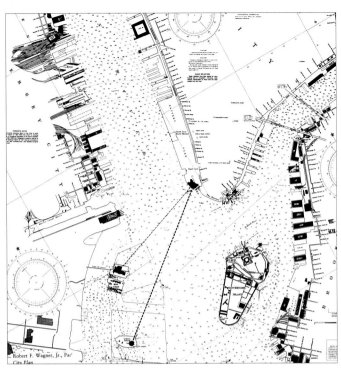

The park in relation
to the geography
of the city

Plan of the blocks to
the south of Battery Park
City and Robert F. Wagner
Jr Park

Aerial view of the park

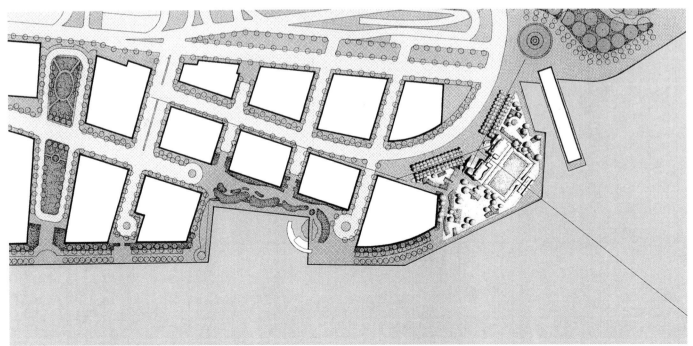

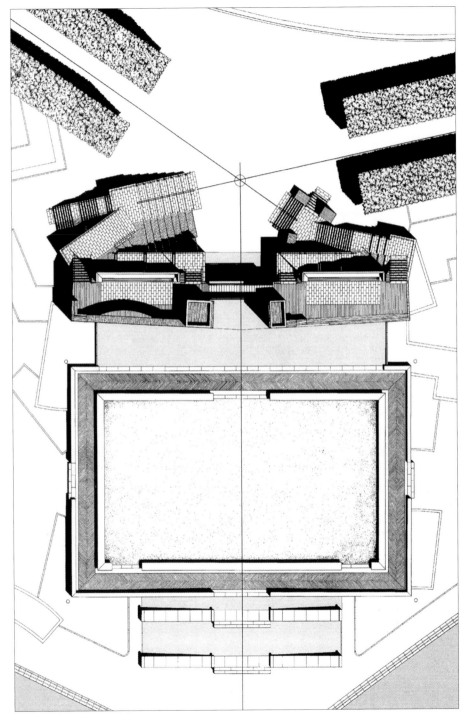

General layout of Robert
F. Wagner Jr Park

Study sketch

Construction details
of the pavilions and
the steps

At pages 84–85:
View from the city
of the pavilions

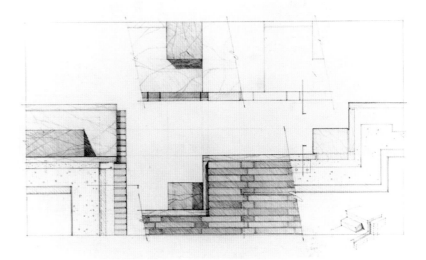

Detail of the seats
at the upper level
of the pavilions

86

Critical Regionalism

Los Angeles, the riots
in 1992

An endless series of wooden houses, nicely kept. A yard surrounding each house, no fence, codified everyday gestures, apparently nothing out of place, the sound of a lawnmower. The gaze digs among the details, it sails along the top of the high grass and stops before a paradoxical detail: a chopped-off ear.

The memorable sequence from David Lynch's *Blue Velvet*[1] revealed, along with other movies from the second half of the Eighties, a setting of the ordinary and everyday riddled with a rising tide of doubts, fears, and uncertainties.

The end of the American Dream, which now dates back at least three decades, the economic crisis of the late Eighties,[2] the fear of that which is alien, different, or anomalous once opened the doors to a process that led slowly to gated neighbourhoods with security guards scattered across the nation, the decline of the collective and community-minded spirit that had always characterize the American province, the flight toward a cartoonish utopia of the *Truman Show*/Seaside and all of its replicas scattered from Florida to California.[3]

One significant element, for example, is the literary success between the end of the Eighties and the early Nineties of two terms like 'new urbanism'[4] and 'sprawl',[5] two characteristics that were most widely used to explain urban phenomena that were diametrically opposes, probably one the direct consequence of the other, and which in both cases at any rate throw into crisis the traditional concept of city and its interpretative instruments.[6] And on the interior of these urban dynamics, which emerge from an interesting evolution of North American society, we can detect one of the elements of greatest continuity in the material history of the United States: the single-family house as an element of resistence and immutability in the American landscape.

In contrast to 'Living Today', an exhibition held in 1998 at MoMA concerning contemporary single-family living, architectural culture displays an apparently irreperable lag with respect to a theme that typologically and structurally remains blocked in nearly all cases in the nineteenth century, even though it has been recently 'gussied up' by Ikea and Wall Paper.

Elements of resistence scattered indifferentiatedly across the deep American province and metropolitan sprawl, transverse from the cultural, economic, and racial point of view and at the same time juxtaposed with a generalized globalization of customs and spaces.

And this is one of the most interesting phenomena of this last decade: the radicalization of a condition in which the globalization of objects, tastes, and flavors is juxtaposed at the same time with a social reaction that has become a search for identity and belonging to a context, masked, from time to time, by the simple folkloric allure from a theme park or strip mall to the learned rediscovery of traditional technologies and materials, from the mystique of space in relation to Mother Earth to the reanalysis of the material and artistic history of native Americans or simply to the reevaluation of one's own roots in a nation that has always boasted an elevated rate of physical mobility and has always encouraged the myth of social mobility.[7]

As far as American architectural culture is concerned, we can discern, as early as the mid-Twenties, a regionalist current with conservative ideological connotations, springing up in California as a reaction to the modern city and the architecture imported passively from the experimentation of the European avant-garde. While a more refined and progressive interpretation of this disorderly reaction to the modern can be identified in Lewis Mumford who, with his writings on regionalism,[8] between the Thirties and the end of the Forties, developed a line of thought that, reevaluating the positive root of the individual context, of its material and environmental history in relation to the quality of life of modern man, inaugurated a 'red line' of post-war

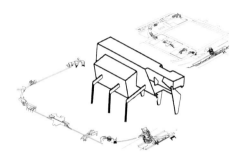

American humanism capable of constructing a 'third way' between modernism and conservatism, respectful of the necessity of people to feel themselves part of a context and of a tradition and at the same time to experience in equilibrium their own modernity.[9]

From the beginning of the Eighties this line of design and theory has been enriched by a major updating defined as 'critical regionalism'[10] which has progressively given visibility to the work of a few young North American architects, among them Stanley Saitowitz, Henry Smith-Miller and Laurie Hawkinson, Patkau, Mark Mack, Williams and Tsien, Antoine Predock, Carlos Jiménez, Arquitectonica, and Steven Holl, whose work, although still on a small scale and especially undertaken in the American 'province', showed a special attention to the environment and the sustainability of architectural design, to a new way of dealing with the concept of community and the physical and sensory quality of built space.[11]

Today we might see this critical operation as an attempt to adjust one's aim with respect to the linguistic and conceptual ambiguities generated by Post-Modernism and, at the same time, to refocus attention on those areas that are distant from the influence of the principal centres of economic and cultural power, seen as realities with a dimension in which it might still be possible to find — through architectural design — a socially useful mediation between modernity and context.

At the beginning of the Nineties this new 'politically correct' variant was counterposed by many critics against the more metropolitan tendencies, 'dirty realism',[12] of the Los Angeles architecture of Frank Gehry, Eric Owen Moss, Morphosis, and Frank Israel, in which the deconstructivist language, consacrated by the umpteenth exhibition curated by Philip Johnson with Mark Wiegly at the MoMA in 1988 as the new languaged of international modernity,[13] marked a clear-eyed and destructive urban architecture with respect to an imploded and ungovernable urban context, probably still marked by the memory of the Los Angeles riots of 1992.

The contemporary evolution of the diverse experiences of the Californian architects, and above all of Owen Moss, Morphosis, and Ro.To., is on the other hand displaying a completely different creative and conceptual attitude in which the projects should not be considered merely structural reactions to the difficulties of metropolitan space but as sensors of a complex reality in which every existing signal is utilized to generate meaning and environmental quality with the materials and signs proper to the metropolis.[14]

One direct demonstration can be seen in the capillary interventions by Owen Moss in Culver City which over the arc of a decade have marked the physical and economic rebirth of this depressed area of Los Angeles, as well as the activity of SCI-Arc[15] during the Nineties as a laboratory of autonomous experiences, deeply rooted in the context of Los Angeles.

In a generalized reality in which 76 percent of the American population is considered urban as against the 46 percent world average, in which Los Angeles county along boasts 9,145,000 inhabitants, or the city of New York boasts a population of 7,380,000,[16] I believe

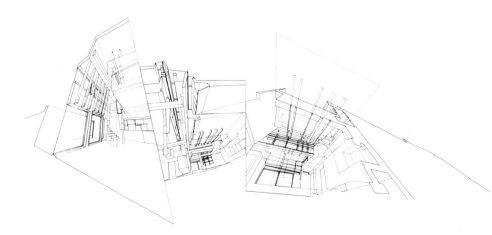

Carlos Jiménez,
Houston Fine Arts Press,
Houston, 1985–87

Williams, Tsien,
Museum of American
Folk Art, New York,
1998–2001

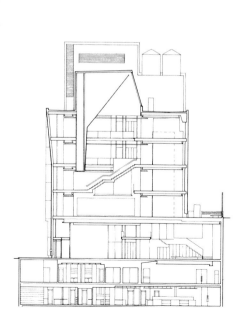

that it is fundamental to begin to consider the contemporary metropolitan condition as a useful paradox, engendering cultural, social, and economic characteristics capable of creating specificities and resources in the urban space.[17]

Many American metropolises have been undergoing an interesting metamorphosis over the last decade, a metamorphosis whose results we can only now begin to analyze. Atlanta, Houston, Seattle, Phoenix, and Boston (to name only a few examples) are undergoing significant changes that have already generated large quantities of architecture built in relation to a series of infrastructural and public-space reforms that are transforming them into de facto contemporary laboratories of great usefulness to understanding the evolution of the urban form in relation to a new, aggressive economic demand and to different social and interethnic pressure.[18]

At the same time, the regionalist experiences noted at the beginning of the Nineties grew in relation to the various architects' artistic development and their context of reference.

Similarly, the very term has evolved that connotes them, which can no longer be considered as an umbrella that accommodates all of the heterodox and regional trends of American architecture.

The discriminating elements are represented today by an attention that places the idea of mental and physical environment at the centre of the design. The built space must correspond to an incessant research that put existing technologies to the test in order to bend them to a concept of sustainable livability, which experiments with new functional and structural typologies in relation to a changing social and economic demand, which interacts

with the natural and historic context by establishing levels of rupture and at the same time trying to reestablish certain links.[19]

The response of contemporary critical regionalism cannot pass through the identification of a language, but rather the definition of processes and a precise mental state.

And many of these examples are closely tied to regional and urban realities undergoing strong expansion in which the growth of new economies of scale are followed by an increase in social demand, investments, and often the reinforcement of educational university structures.

This is especially the case of states like Nevada, Texas, and New Mexico, realities that have benefited directly from the NAFTA agreements of 1993, a uniform flow of immigration, and new investments in the field of information technologies.

The experiences of Antoine Predock, Will Bruder, Lake/Flato Architects, Ricardo Legorreta, and Ten Arquitectos and Carlos Jiménez in the south-west of the United States[20] are testimonials to this interesting regional evolution and to the determination to find a scale of relation between light modernity, the respect for the environment and for local traditions, and a sensory and spiritual quality of public and private architectural space.

[1] *Blue Velvet*, directed by David Lynch, 120', USA 1986.
[2] *An Age of Anxiety*, in Various authors, *America's History*, Philadelphia, Worth Publ., 1997, pp. 1030–41.
[3] Dietmar M. Steiner, 'The Truman Show', in *Domus*, no. 818, June 1999, pp. 8–9.
[4] For one of the most complete analyses of New American Urbanism, see: John Dutton, *The New American Urbanism*, Milan, Skira, 2000.
[5] Concerning the concept of 'sprawl', we would mention the

Carlos Jiménez,
renovation and expansion
on the Nelson Atkins
Museum, Kansas City,
Missouri, 1999

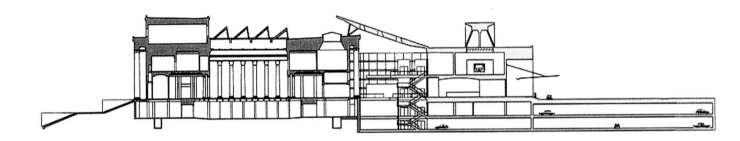

Patkau, Seabird Island
School, Agassiz, British
Columbia (Canada),
1988–91

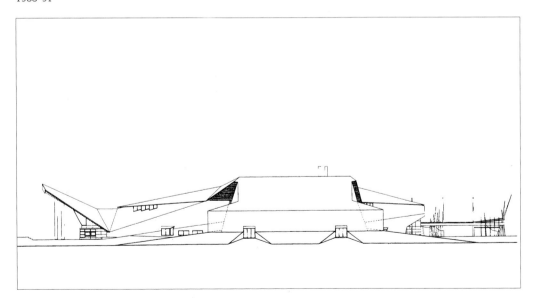

numerous public writings and lectures by Richard Ingersoll during the Nineties, still awaiting definitive publication.

[6] Among the various volumes that have appeared on the crisis of the contemporary American city and its redefinition, we recommend: Michael Sorkin (edited by), *A Variation on a Theme Park: the New American City and the End of Public Space,* Farrar, Straus & Giroux, 1991; Joan Copjer, Michael Sorkin (edited by), *Giving Ground: the Politics of Propinquity*, New Left Books, 1999.

[7] 'Misunderstandings about the "American city" stem from misconceptions about the American mentality that produced it.' André Corboz in an enlightening pamphlet on American cities dismantles many of the commonplaces that have circulated throughout the twentieth century among European critics, explaining also the difficulties in understanding American urban phenomena. And one of the passages concerns precisely the supposed absence of roots and the historical amnesia of the Americans, a cliché that has always intersected with the country's strong social mobility. André Corboz, *Looking for a City in America*, Los Angeles, The Getty Center for the History of Art and the Humanities, 1992, pp. 55–56.

[8] See: Lewis Mumford, *The South in Architecture*, New York, Harcourt, Brace & Company, 1941; Alexander Tzonis, Liane Lefaivre, 'Lewis Mumford's Regionalism', in *Design Book Review*, no. 19, 1991, pp. 20–25; Alexander Tzonis, Liane Lefaivre, Richard Diamond, *Architecture in North America since 1960*, London, Thames and Hudson, 1995, pp. 13–19, and Michela Rosso, Paolo Scrivano, *Introduzione*, in Lewis Mumford, *La cultura della città,* Turin, Edizioni di Comunità, 1999.

[9] Alexander Tzonis, Liane Lefaivre, Richard Diamond, *op. cit.*, pp. 10–38.

[10] The term 'critical regionalism' was used for the first time by Alexander Tzonis and Liane Lefaivre in 'The Grid and the Pathway', in *Architecture in Greece*, no. 5, 1981; subsequently the same authors and Kenneth Frampton expanded on this concept and spread it widely. In this connection, see: Alexander Tzonis, Liane Lefaivre, *Critical Regionalism*, in Spyros Amourgis (edited by), *Critical Regionalism: the Pomona Meeting Proceedings*, California State Polytechnic University, Pomona, 1991, pp. 1–27, and

Alexander Tzonis, Liane Lefaivre, Richard Diamond, *op. cit.*, pp. 51–54; Kenneth Frampton, *Towards a Critical Regionalism*, in H. Foster (edited by), *The Anti-Aesthetic*, Port Townsend, Bay Press, 1983; 'Zabriskie Point: la Traiettoria di un sonnambulo', in *Casabella*, no. 586-587, January-February 1992, pp. 8–13, and 'L'America Incognita: un'antologia', in *Casabella*, no. 607, December 1993, pp. 50–67.

[11] Alexander Tzonis, Liane Lefaivre, Richard Diamond, *op. cit.*, p. 51.

[12] Concerning the concept of 'dirty realism', see the various writings of Liane Lefaivre, including: 'L'Architecture du réalisme hideux', in *Carrè Bleu*, no. 2, 1988, pp. 31–36; 'Otro realismo sucio', in *Arquitectura viva*, no. 3, November 1988, pp. 9–15, and Alexander Tzonis, Liane Lefaivre, Richard Diamond, *op. cit.*, pp. 55–57.

[13] Philip Johnson, Mark Wiegly (edited by), *Deconstructivist Architecture*, New York, MoMA, 1988.

[14] Edward Soja, 'Lessons in Spatial Justice', in *Hunch*, no. 1, 1999, pp. 98–107.

[15] Michael Rotondi, Margaret Reeve (edited by)*, From the Center: Design Process at SCI-Arch*, New York, Monacelli Press, 1996.

[16] *Cities*, in Richard Saul Wurman (edited by), *Understanding USA*, Tedx, R. R. Donnelley & Sons, 2000.

[17] In this connection, see the last three books by Mike Davies, an attempt to analyze Los Angeles as a complex structure: *City of Quartz: Excavating the Future in Los Angeles*, Random House, 1992; *Ecology of Fear: Los Angeles and the Imagination of Disaster*, Henry Holt 1998 and *Magical Urbanism: Latinos Reinvent the US City*, Verso Publ., 2000.

[18] In this connection, see the recent essay by Sanford Qwinter for the exhibition 'Mutations'. Sanford Qwinter, Daniela Fabricius, *The American City*, in Various authors, *Mutations*, Barcelona, Actar, 2000, pp. 484–649.

[19] In this connection, see the interesting development in the critical work of Kenneth Frampton who worked his way from the notion of *Critical Regionalism* to the more overall idea of *Tectonics*. Kenneth Frampton, *Studies in Tectonic Culture*, Cambridge (Mass.), MIT Press, 1996.

[20] Diane Ghirado, 'A proposito dell'architettura del Sudovest', in *Lotus*, no. 102, pp. 116–30.

American Heritage Center and Art Museum, Laramie, Wyoming, 1987–93

Antoine Predock

General layout

Access to the third-floor terrace

Built at the edge of the campus of the University of Wyoming, the American Heritage Center, created as a research institute as well as a museum space in which to house the different art collections of the university, seems to summarize several of the characteristics of the more recent design work of Antoine Predock.

It is a monumental sign capable of measuring itself directly with the surrounding natural landscape. A composition of forms and elementary geometries in which matter, light, and symbolism are fused through an essential thought. This is an ordering element of the territory, in which the hierarchies of the interior and exterior space interpenetrate, generating a building of great structural rigour and, at the same time, of great emotional evocativeness.

In this project, as in the more recent Spencer Theater in Alto (1997) and the Arizona Science Center in Phoenix (1997), we can clearly see efforts to reconcile the path of critical regionalism, the lessons of Kahn and Barragán, and at the same time, the perception of architecture as a monumental element engaged in a direct dialogue with the sublime aspect of the American natural landscape.

The complex, raised by terracing with respect to the surrounding parking areas, is made up of two buildings joined to compose an L shape that opens onto the open-air sculpture courtyard.

The large pyramid of the research centre, clad in copper, and the low curtain wall made of cement blocks of the museum are structured according to an east-west axis marked, according to the original project, by a symbolic sequence offered by the large fireplace set at the centre of the cone, by the sculpture terrace, and lastly by a pavilion from which to view the rising sun.

Symbolic and functional structure overlay each other easily through a very interesting use of geometries and spatial sequencing.

A diagonal line with respect to the principal orientation leads via a ramp from the parking areas to the hall which communicates simultaneously with the museum and the research centre, the former organized with a central corridor that distributes to the various exhibition halls, the latter on the other hand extending vertically with a system of spaces for study set around a large fireplace, a true *axis mundi* caged in a reticular structure of wood and cement.

Certain elements serve as sensory guides on the interior of the building, from the two fireplaces set at the centre of the cone and at the end of the corridor that distributes the museum, to the various wells and skylights that channel and shape the light, taking up several structural themes present in traditional American architecture.

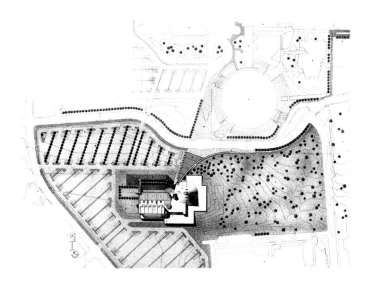

Axonometric projection
and functional distribution
of the complex

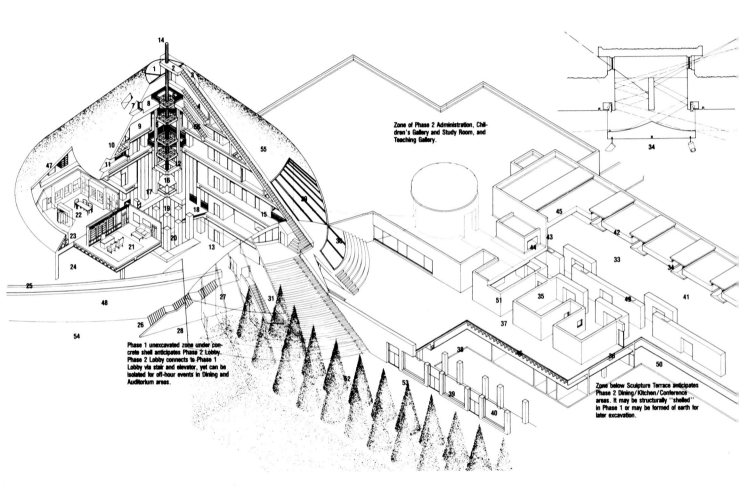

Zone of Phase 2 Administration, Children's Gallery and Study Room, and Teaching Gallery.

Phase 1 unexcavated zone under concrete shell anticipates Phase 2 Lobby. Phase 2 Lobby connects to Phase 1 Lobby via stair and elevator, yet can be isolated for off-hour events in Dining and Auditorium areas.

Zone below Sculpture Terrace anticipates Phase 2 Dining/Kitchen/Conference areas. It may be structurally "shelled" in Phase 1 or may be formed of earth for later excavation.

The pyramid

Cross-section
of the pyramid

Nocturnal view of the
pyramid and the sculpture
garden

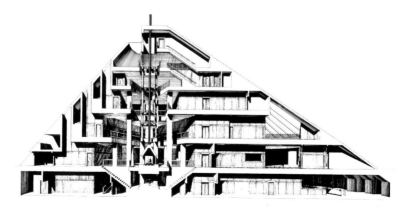

Ground floor

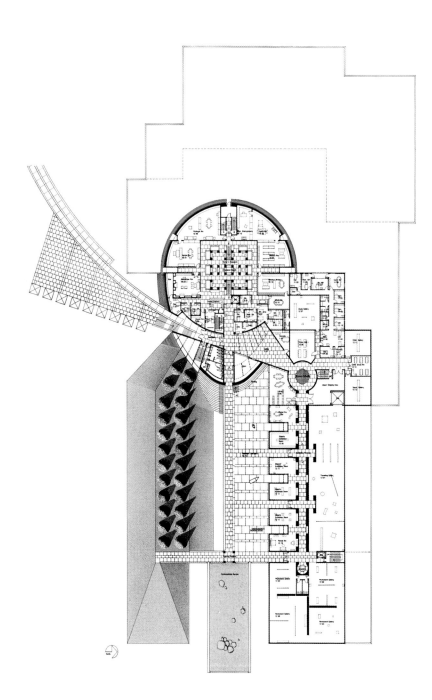

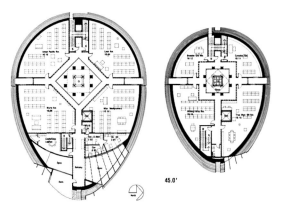

45.0'

Sculpture garden

Exhibition hall
on the ground floor

57.0'

67.0'

77.0'

Entrance hall
of the pyramid

The smoke stack and
the upper structure
of the central furnace

Central furnace
on the ground floor
of the pyramid

105

Central Library, Phoenix, Arizona, 1989–95

bruderDWLarchitects
Collaborator: W. Burnett

The new Central Library of Phoenix presents itself as an anomalous body on the interior of the city.

Isolated, solidly anchored to the earth, possessed of a powerful material and structural personality, it seems more that it is seeking a dialogue with the great mountains that wreath the city area than with the few skyscrapers that punctuate the centre of Phoenix.

The building is located, along with the new Phoenix Art Museum designed by Williams and Tsien between 1991 and 1996, in an area at the end of Central Avenue, the main thoroughfare that is lined by the most important and impressive buildings of the urban centre, and which seems to be concluded by the library itself, with its monumental presence.

A civil architecture, designed for the city and to offer the best possible spatial quality in which to read, to study, and to examine books.

The new Central Library presents itself as an 'ark' that offers a bulwark against the noise of the adjoining street and at the same time ensures the best conditions of light and environment to the reader.

The body of the building is organized according to an elementary structural and functional scheme in which two side 'pockets' are applied to the central rectangular 'box' dedicated to reading and books; these two side 'pockets' contain services and secondary access to the various floors.

The design of the façades and the very sequence of the interior spaces, then, follow this principle with the two long eastern and western fronts screened with a differentiated system of copper panelling and interrupted vertically by a steel facing that marks the entrance to the library. The two short sides, slightly set back with respect to the copper façades, are instead completely glassed in an screened with a system of sails on the north side and by mechanical devices to regulate the sunlight on the south.

The two glassed-in fronts reveal the soul of the library, the system of its public spaces, and above all the great reading room locating on the top floor.

Access to the central rooms of the library is skillfully calibrated through a sequence in which the use of different materials, colours, and the spatial characteristics of the building are juggled, revealing a profound understanding of classical architecture and at the same time of nature as a source of sublime emotions.

The two entrances, built along the same axis and slightly lowered with respect to the interior floor level, lead us into a dark tunnel that then leads to the central hall, a veritable artificial canyon illuminated by the natural light that beats down from the skylights in the ceiling, caged within the system of starways and the main elevators, encased in a grand glass prism.

The vertigo of the hall makes it possible to take in at a single glance the internal organization of the library, its simple structure, and the world of books that glitter from on high.

Steel, reinforced concrete, and glass interact directly with the green, red, and yellow tones that characterize the surfaces and the furniture, also designed by Bruder.

The sequence of floors leads progressively from the second floor, dedicated to the children's library and to the area for bibliographic research and the periodicals sections, to the third floor — administrative offices — and to the fourth floor, as a space for lectures, also housing the Arizona Collection, all the way up to the top floor, which houses only the reading room.

And in this great space that crowns the library, one perceives, as in the entrance lobby, the characteristics that regulated the overall design of the building.

The visitor can embrace in a single glance a space with the classical proportions and rhythm that evoke the spatiality of the libraries of Labrouste and which, at the same time, is enveloped in a natural light filtering down from the large skylights.

The grid of pillars in reinforced concrete punctuates the hall, which looks north and south with grand glassed walls over the city, and especially overlooks the surrounding ring of mountains.

And in the point of natural contact between the ceiling and the pillars, Bruder creates the last, and most powerful tension: the tip of the pillars, treated in steel, does not touch the ceiling, unloading all of the structural tensions with a system of steel cables that attaches directly to the side walls. The pillars look directly onto the skylights, which present a small glass oculus that allows a beam of sunlight to filter through only on the occasion of the summer solstice, intensely heating the steel tip.

A contemporary *axis mundi* that attempts to tie a modern building to the earth and its history.

Detail of the sunshade of the north façade

View of the south elevation from Central Avenue

1

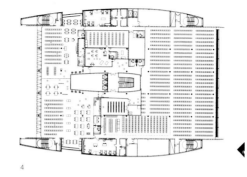

4

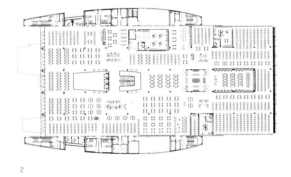

2

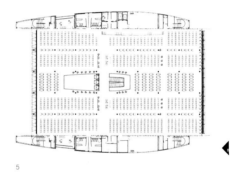

5

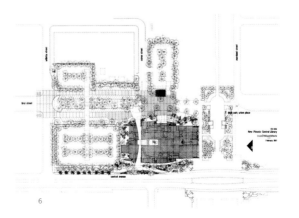

3

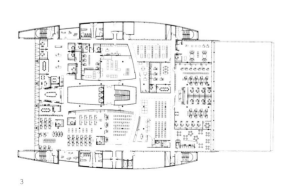

6

1. Ground floor

2. Second floor

3. Third floor

4. Fourth floor

5. Fifth floor

6. General layout.
Library and parking

View of the north
elevation

Longitudinal cross-section

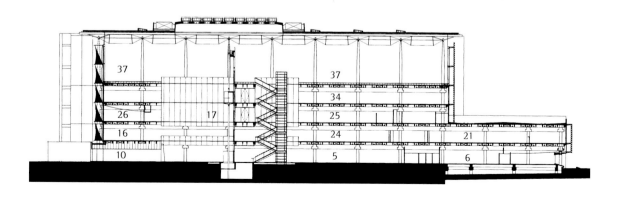

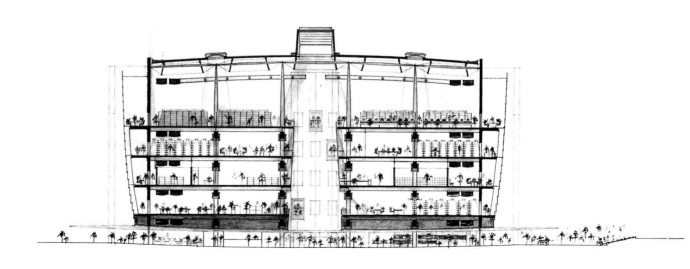

Detail of the reading room
on the fifth floor

Study sketch.
Detail of the skylight
in its relation to the pillar
beneath it

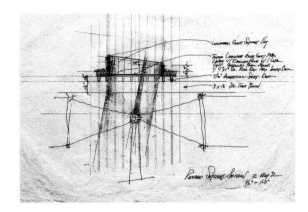

Strawberry Vale Elementary School, Victoria, British Columbia, Canada, 1992–95

Patkau
John and Patricia Patkau with G. Cheung,
M. Cunningham, M. Kothke, T. Newton,
D. Shone, P. Suter, J. Wang

Ever since the very first residential designs and small-scale public works by Patkau that reached from the 'distant provinces of the empire' at the beginning of the Nineties, it was possible to sense the power of a silent research that quested tirelessly to join the contemporary with a natural context and a rereading of traditional local architecture.

The design and construction of the Strawberry Vale Elementary School in Victoria seems a perfect distillation of this creative and ideological process.

The new school building was built at the edges of a school compound that had grown progressively, beginning from the little schoolhouse built in 1893, to which was added a second building in the Fifties, right up to the acquisition, meant for a new installation, of a parcel of land further to the south, overlooking the edges of Rosedale Park, an expanse dovered with delicate white oaks.

An enclosure located at the outskirts of the city in a largely natural setting, dotted with small single-family homes.

And it was with this context that the new project confronted itself and established a dialogue.

The new school developed initially as a piece of land design, placing great importance on the topography, on the drainage of water and at the same time, the micro-environment existing around the park. The building was designed beginning from a preordained functional program which called for a structure of 3,292 square metres for sixteen classrooms, a library, a gymnasium, educational spaces, and administrative offices.

The semi-rural character of the surrounding context influenced the organization of the general layout, with the collective and administrative spaces looking to the north toward the parking area and the entry road, while the system of the classrooms was exposed on the south side, toward the park.

The classrooms, organized in groups of four, presented themselves as autonomous pavilions depending upon the main core of the building in accordance with a sequence made up of small, progressive shifts capable of creating on the one hand a system of free internal spaces straddling the classrooms and the traditional collective places, and on the other hand of offering a visual contact and a direct access to the park.

The general section perfectly rendered the hierarchic character of the spaces, in the relationship among the classrooms, with a long roof sloping down toward the woods, and the high central space, the distributive vertebral column of the entire layout.

In this project, as in the previous Seabird Island School at Agassiz (1988–91), the roof took on a fundamental role in supplying a strong identity to the design as well as serving as a symbolic link with North American vernacular architecture.

The construction materials were selected according to local traditions and their availability on sight, at once paying close attention to energy saving and to the reduction of components that might potentially be toxic to users of the school.

Wood, therefore, was used both for load-bearing structures and for the interior and exterior facings, while steel, reinforced concrete, and wall facings were applied to support the principal structure and to improve the energy and sensory quality of the interior spaces.

Eastern front

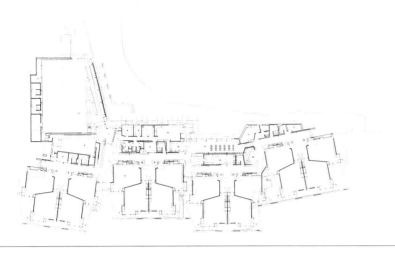

Plan of the ground floor

The wooden structure
in relation to the plan

Plan of the roofs

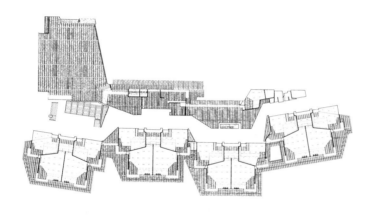

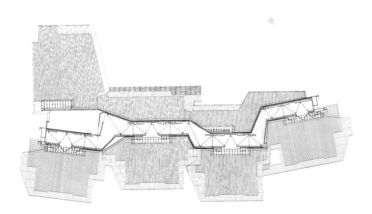

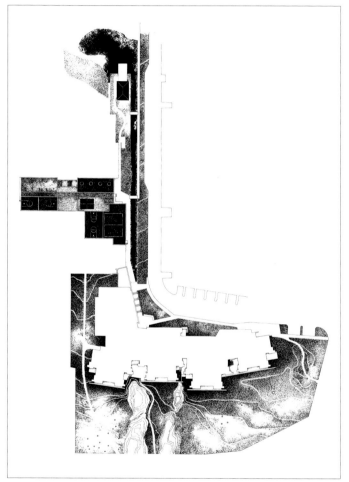

Entrance and presidential
offices

View of the park

View of the park from
one of the passageways
between the blocks
of classrooms

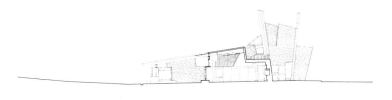

Transverse cross-sections, classrooms to the east and exterior covered spaces (top and centre), library and spaces reserved for personnel (bottom)

Transverse cross-section, classrooms and workshops

Longitudinal cross-section, classrooms, and gymnasium

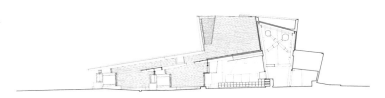

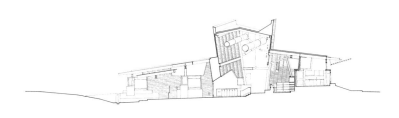

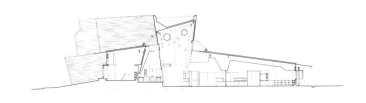

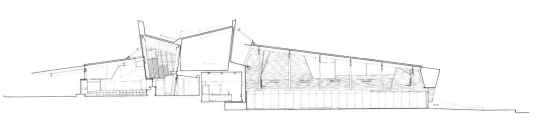

Detail of the plan of the
classrooms in relation to
the hallway and collective
spaces

Interior of a classroom

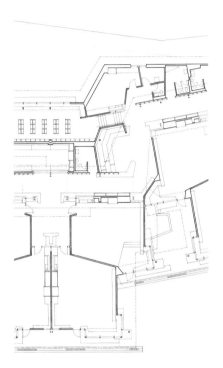

Carlson-Reges Residence, Los Angeles, California, 1992–95

Ro.To. Architects
Michael Rotondi and Clark Stevens
with A. Hiltz, K. Kim, Y. Obuchi, B. Reiff, C. Scott

The context: an industrial building in Neoclassical style built at the turn of the century by the first agency for electric power in Los Angeles. A building in the middle of a metropolitan area bordering downtown L.A., surrounded by industrial buildings, warehouses for construction material, and by a heavy-transport railroad line.

The clients: a couple consisting of an art expert and collector and a builder and developer with special expertise in the disposal and recycling of heavy construction materials.

The process of creation and construction that led to the execution of this project, therefore, came about in the sign of a determination to intervene and nevertheless preserve and exalt the soul of the place while, at the same time, from a relationship between the designers and the clients considered as an engendering source of a continuous work in progress capable of stimulating and enriching the architectural project.

The house was in fact built by the client's firm and with direct intervention on the part of the client; moreover several of the elements characterizing the project develop as a creative reutilization of construction materials already in the possession of the owner.

The difficult environmental nature of the context was confronted with a notable propensity to listen on the part of the designer, the outskirts of town were not seen as a site to be ignored but rather as an environment whose signs should be considered and used.

The transition from public building to private and domestic place was resolved with the construction of a steel wall hanging in space and directly hooked to the new roof, to protect the house from the noise of the adjoining railroad, as well as to create the first of a series of intimate spaces between the interior and the exterior that punctuate the path through the villa.

The change is declared through the addition to the existing building of a new story which becomes the roof and at the same appropriates the sides of the old building.

The sequence of interior spaces, on the other hand, is organized as a gentle flow of interior and exterior places with a garden, where the domestic route allows the progressive unveiling of the spaces of the house and, at the same time, the perception of guided views of the surrounding city.

The entrance on the ground floor is organized in the shade of the large steel panel protecting the house from the railroad, and it incorporates the main stairway of the house which distributes to the different floors and to a series of raised catwalks that move around the domestic spaces.

The ground floor revolves around the studio, which houses the art collection, and the garden, while the first level is developed so as to exalt the visual link between the interior and exterior with the large double-height living room, overlooked by the night zone, and which communicates directly with the terrace and the pool.

This large wooden deck which looks directly toward downtown was designed together with the pool, built with the use of an old steel cistern which is suspended over the garden below, and which is also fastened directly to the living room in the house.

Metal fixtures and elements treated with wood and coloured plaster define the nature of a residential space that does not ignore the harshness of the surrounding landscape and which at the same time attempts to define the characteristics of a harmonious domesticity, aware of its contemporary nature.

The house seen from the interior garden

The house, the
surrounding buildings,
and downtown
Los Angeles

The new version
compared with
the previously existing
building

Conceptual scheme
of the existing building

Conceptual scheme
of the project

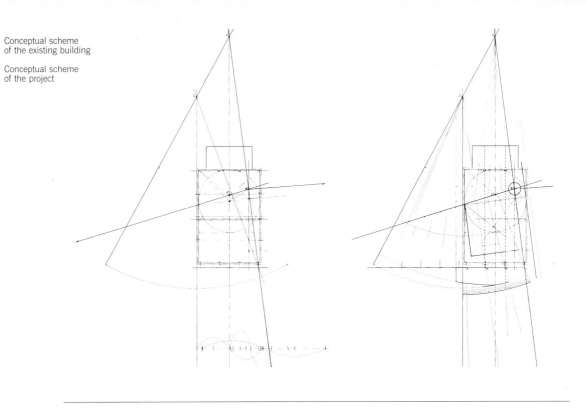

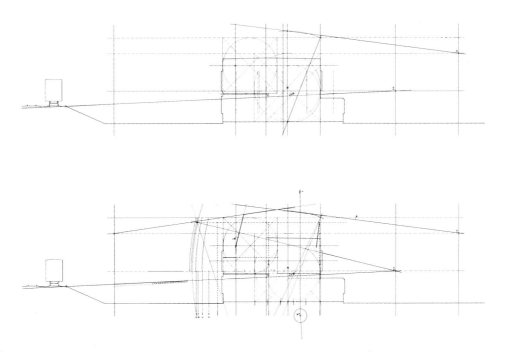

Ground floor   Transverse cross-section

Second floor   Longitudinal cross-section

Third floor

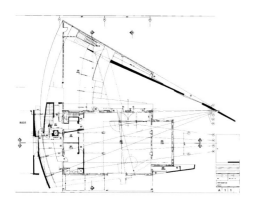

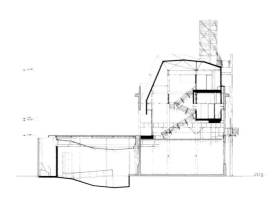

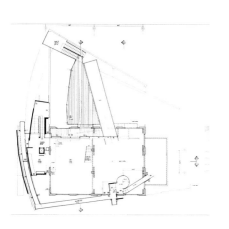

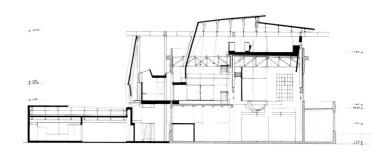

External catwalk
on the second floor
and the noise-proof
barrier

The interior garden
and the hanging pool

The atelier on the ground
floor and overlook
on the hanging pool

The new roof seen
from the interior

The night zone
on the third floor

Double-height living room
on the second floor

Diamond Ranch High School,
Los Angeles, California,
1993–2000

Morphosis
Thom Mayne with C. Crockett, D. Grant,
F. Kremkus, J. Shimizu, P.J. Tighe

The problem, by now generally felt, of designing a new public building in a semi-peripheral area was faced by Morphosis with the definition of a sign that would represent at once an act of foundation and a link with the existing ground.

The topography, the elevations, and the slopes of a territory that had survived urbanization and was at the same time besieged by certain powerful signs of manmade progress such as fast highways, water channels, electric lines, allowed the designers in any case to identify and anchor their work to a series of strong elements capable of inspiring part of the design approaches.

The identification of these elements of epiphany was followed by a further reflection on the very meaning of a building for a public school in the United States, seen as an act capable of affirming a precise cultural and ideological determination, that would transform this project for a high school into a significant response with respect to the debate and the production underway.

In a phase of history in which much of America's architectural culture is involved in the reformulation and design of university structures, extraordinary importance attaches to the reference made by Morphosis to the renovation of school buildings from previous educational phases, used by a more substantial and socially differentiated number of students.

The architecture of schools as a diffuse experience of the contemporary and, at the same time, of spatial quality: this seems to be the reference that reaches us from this recent project by the Los Angeles-based studio.

The school complex is organized along a series of terracings that, running parallel, accommodate the two main clusters of buildings, the upper block of the gymnasium, the library, the workshops, and the administrative offices, and the lower block of the schoolrooms, which overlook a long central 'road'.

The flow of students is thus accommodated by this unprecedented urban environment, a meeting place, identity of the new building and at the same time theatrical depiction, 'under the open sky', of scholastic life.

The sequence of buildings is designed in fact according to a logic dictated by the determination to construct an 'urban experience' for the students: from the entrance that overlooks the parking area, in which the two blocks of buildings seem to touch to protect the stairway leading up and in to the campus, to the gradual uncovering of the interior road that distributes to the two orders of levels and which offers at the same time unexpected views of the surrounding landscape.

The same system of distributive spaces is organized as a syncopated sequence of gardens, ramps, meeting places, and roads, as in the case of the block of schoolrooms, full-fledged pieces of building launched into the void of the valley beneath, and served through small courtyards equipped with ramps that move around the protected green areas toward the exterior.

On the upper and lower levels of the buildings the playing fields are located, a sort of cushion between the school and the exterior reality.

The space alludes without ever dropping into the caricature of the traditional urban environment, while the buildings are resolved with a rigorous use of language and materials, poor in details and founded on the force of the volumes and their orchestration.

The interior road
of the school

Model

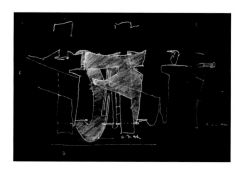

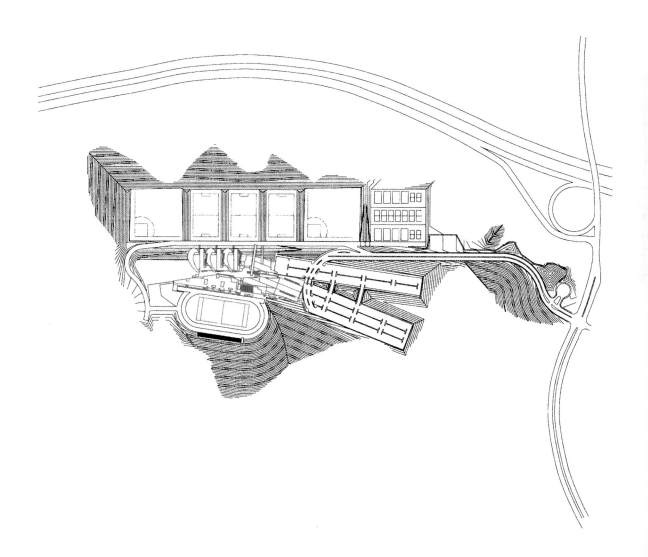

Plan of the first level

Plan of the second level

Plan of the third level

Plan of the roofs

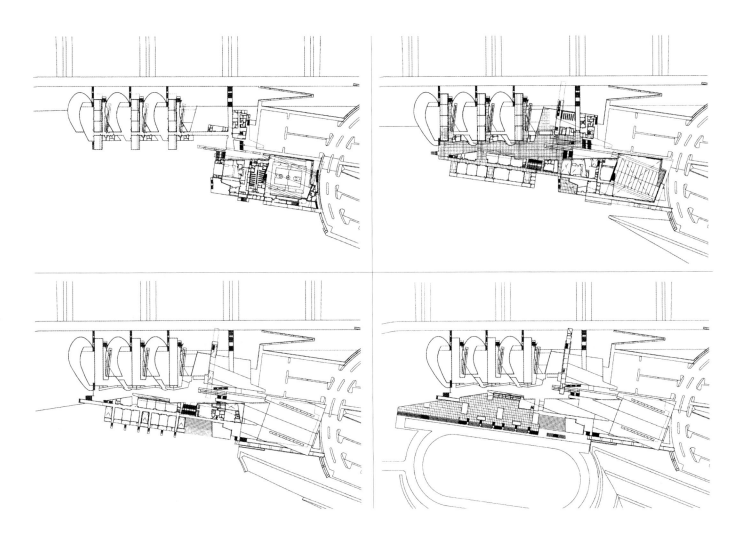

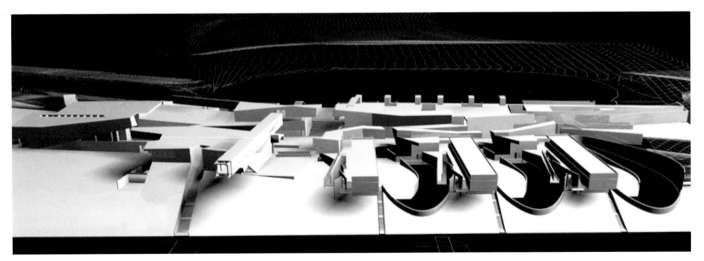

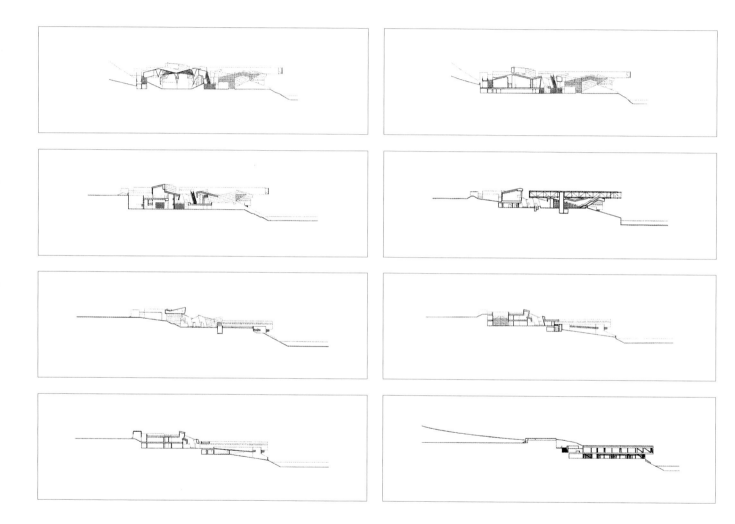

Relationship among
the various blocks
of the school

Model of the overall
structure, detail

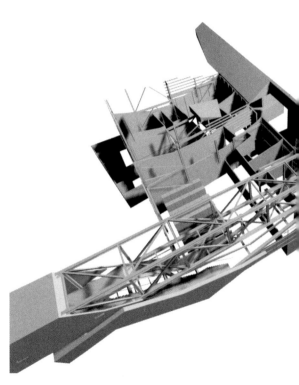

The gymnasium

Entrance to the halls

Samitaur, Culver City, California, 1990–96

Eric Owen Moss
Project architects: J. Vanos, D. Ige

The period straddling the end of the Eighties and the early Nineties can be considered a turning point for the creative development and the professional success of Eric Owen Moss.

His meeting in 1989 with the developer Frederick Norton Smith gave birth, in fact, to an interesting urban experience in the history of Los Angeles, which corresponded to the progressive reconversion of a substantial part of Culver City, one of the most central and run-down areas of mid-town Los Angeles, transformed into one of the new centres destinated to house workshops and agencies linked to the world of advertising and film.

But it is not so much in the functional reconversion of this urban area that we should seek the value of new things, as much as in the continual typological and spatial experimentation carried forward by Owen Moss on fragments of Culver City, capable of revealing after a decade a plan of urban reform conceived as a work in progress, able of influencing the transformation of this entire urban area.

The starting point of this story is the project undertaken for the Samitaur, an office building conceived as an addition and at the same time a courageous metamorphosis of an existing industrial building.

The theme: the need of a client, an agency for the processing of digital images, to have more space for offices and workshops in an area filled with warehouses and small industrial buildings organized around a secondary road.

The limitations: an expanse of land crossed by a road with necessary passage of trucks for loading and unloading. It was therefore necessary to plan on a minimum clearance of 4.5 metres of height, along with a regulatory plan that limited the total height of buildings to 14.5 metres, and a prohibition from the fire department to support structures on existing buildings.

Owen Moss proposed an apparently daring solution that was innovative in typological terms: a block running 100 metres in length suspended above the road and the existing buildings, fastened to a system of steel pillars and beams that rest directly on the ground or which unload onto the existing structures of the buildings beneath them.

At the same time, the existing buildings were reconverted into new areas for workshops and offices with a few substantial modifications.

The new building structure, organized on two floors with future plans to climb still higher, presented itself with a linear front marked in the terminal areas by two stairwells treated as strongly sculptural elements, powerful signals of the new intervention on the interior of an apparently anonymous urban area.

Both these interventions play with the staging of a new formal and plastic narrative, a shock — internal to the project itself — that condenses and unveils tensions and memories, attracting the gaze of the visitor to the interior and at the same time referring to an unprecedented visual and tactile relationship with the surrounding landscape and the material of the architecture.

The end of the buildings, shaped like a hollowed-out cone, marks the new entrance to the covered road for trucks and cars and channels one of the pedestrian ramps, while in the northern end an open-air pentagonal empty space unveils a double-height lecture space which opens a fissure in the main façade, revealing the interior mechanism of the architecture.

Study sketch

View of the Samitaur
in relation to the
surrounding landscape

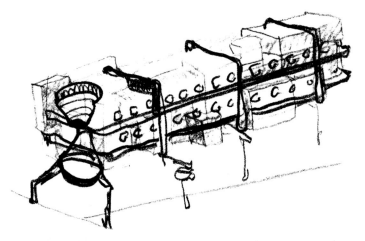

View of the Samitaur
in relation to the
surrounding buildings

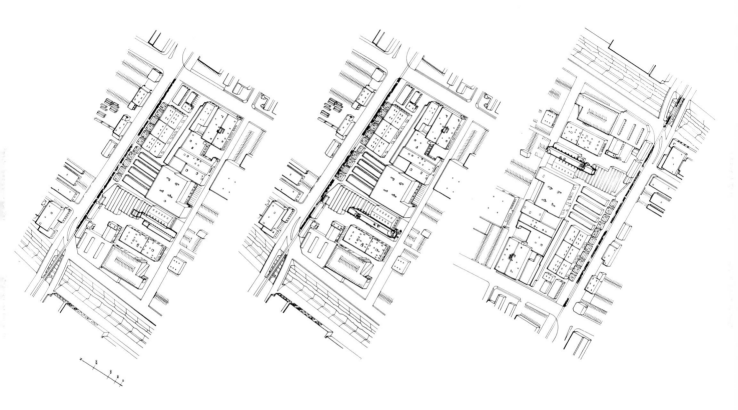

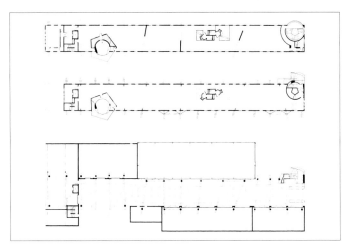

Plans of the ground floor,
first floor, and third floor

Longitudinal and
transverse cross-sections

Axonometric projection
of the second floor

Axonometric cross-section
of the structure

View of the interior road
on the ground floor

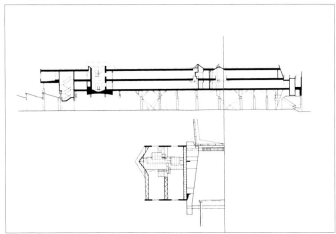

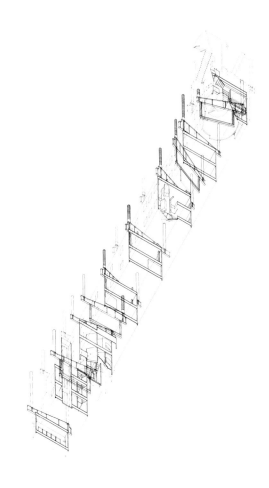

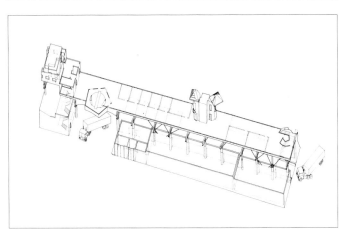

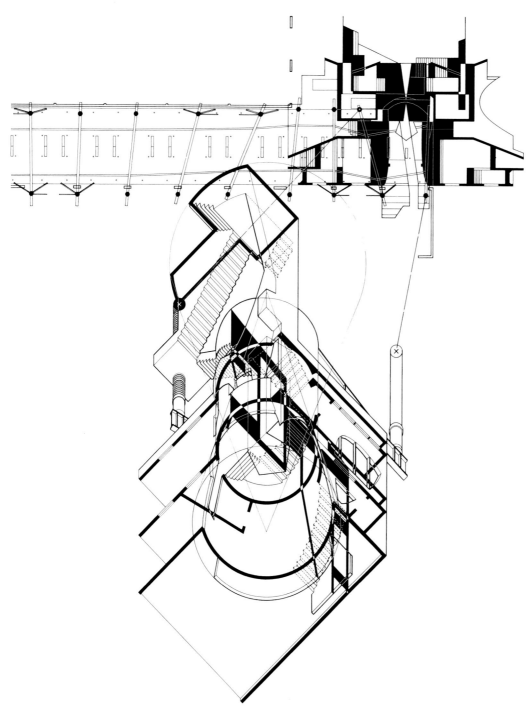

Axonometric cross-section
of the south stairwell

Detail of the circular
stairwell from the interior

Detail of the ground floor
in relation to the external
space

Detail of the north-west
façade

Axonometric cross-section
of the stairwell and the
lecture space

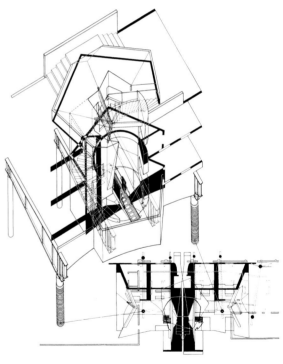

Study sketch

View from the top
of the pentagonal stairwell

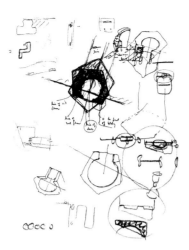

Saint Ignatius Chapel, Seattle, Washington, 1994–97

Steven Holl

Built on a very limited budget, the chapel of Saint Ignatius is located on the edge of a university campus, composing — with the large basin building just in front of the entrance and with a future grassy rectangle on the north side — a major expansion of the university toward the surrounding city.

Holl responded to the potential scarsity of economic resources by utilizing light and colour as hierarchic and symbolic elements internal to the chapel.

Natural lights with different heights, densities, and forms to mark the route to the faithful, moving from the nave (yellow field with a blue lens and blue field with yellow lens) to the narthex or forecourt (natural light), from the processional space (natural light) to the tabernacle (orange field with red lens), the choir (green field in red lens), and the chapel of Reconciliation (red field in orange lens).

The stained glass windows become the final element of the various structural elements of the church, large skylights conceived as veritable 'bottles of light'.

Since actual coloured glass would have been too expensive, Holl made use of a 'series of coloured fields with reflectors painted on the reverse and, at the centre of each one, a single piece of glass in a complementary colour'.

The entire building was constructed, again because of budget concerns, by utilizing slabs of concrete. Twenty-one slabs mounted and fit together in two days, in accordance with a design that harmonizes the various façades in an abstract interplay of signs and apertures that reinforce its warp and weft.

The complexity and practically byzantine refinement displayed on the exterior melt on the interior of the chapel into a calibrated relationship among the paths, the various liturgical spaces marked by the colours of the stained glass windows, by the treatment of the surfaces, and by the furnishings designed by the architect.

A material grace already found in the domestic projects and the designs of small exhibition spaces in the early Nineties, reminiscent of the lesson of Scarpa and, at the same time, the mystique of religious spaces of Le Corbusier. Nevertheless, this small chapel proposes itself as a constructive and compositional theme of great interest already explored on a grand scale in the projects for Fukuoka and for the new dormitories at MIT in Cambridge, currently in the final planning stages.

The chapel and
the university campus

The chapel and
the existing buildings

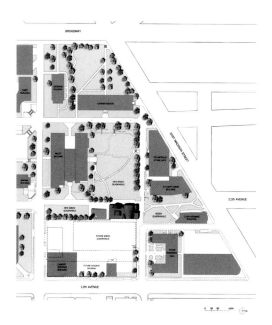

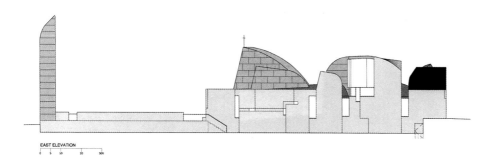

EAST ELEVATION
0 5 10 20 30ft

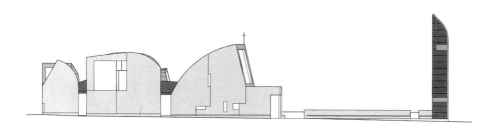

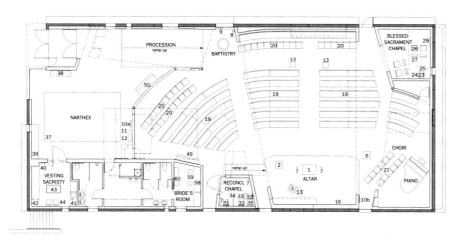

Assembly of the
prefabricated panels made
of reinforced concrete

Western front

Longitudinal
cross-sections,
total and partial

Study sketch

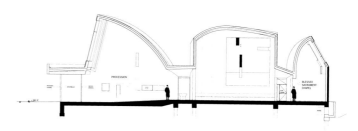

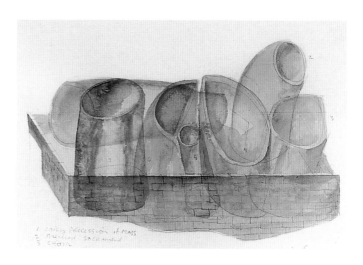

Transverse
cross-sections

Detail of the western front

The bell tower and
the water basin seen
from the interior
of the chapel

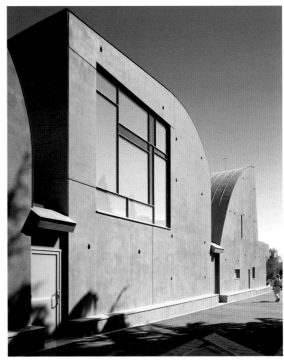

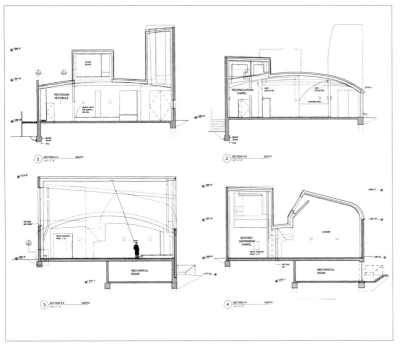

Altar and the principal
space for religious
functions

Single-Family House, New York, 1993–94

Williams, Tsien and Associates
Collaborator: V. Wang

A profound vertical of natural light and a wall that defends the domestic hearth from the exterior; we could thus describe this unusual single-family residence built on East Seventy-Second Street in New York during the first half of the Nineties.

A remarkable project for a fairly drab period of construction in New York and, at the same time, an original typological reinterpretation of the single-family urban house of the upper middle class of the nineteenth century.

The lot, with dimensions of 9 x 30 metres, was obtained through the demolition of two modest buildings dating from the turn of the twentieth century.

The new intervention, literally clamped between two tradition brick and stone constructions of different sizes, stands in total autonomy with respect to the street frontage with a façade that limits to the greatest degree possible the apertures and which is concluded by the large skylight atop it all.

A theme that we shall see again a few years later in the recent project, of the Museum of American Folk Art in New York, which features a very similar relationship between the closed façade on the street, the interior cross-section, and the use of natural light, with a more in-depth study of the theme of the exterior skin with an experimental use of a treatment in white bronze (Tombasil) with an artisanal finish.

The façade on the street presents itself primarily as a result of the interior *Raumplan*, a very linear vertical section that establishes a sequence of fairly traditional domestic spaces, from the pool in the sub-basement floor and on to the kitchen, the first living room, and the dining room on the ground floor. Next comes, on the second floor, the large double-height living room, integrated by the library and the master study; the mezzanine houses the guest area while on the top two floors are the night zones for the family and for the domestic staff.

The orderly sequence of spaces is regulated by the great stairway set at the centre of the building, which revolves around a monumental wall which serves as a slide for the light in the night zone, all the way to the pool below. Just as the façade on the street is hermetically sealed, likewise on the interior side overlooking a little garden measuring 9 x 9 metres there opens a large glassed front that declares the sequence of the interior spaces. The elegant layout of the façades is reinforced by a constant care in the design of the fixtures and in the use of the materials utilized, which recurs in the design of all the interior details, from the furniture to the carpets in the living room.

Study sketch for the façade on the street

Façade on the street

172

Façade on the private
garden

Basement and pool   Ground floor

Second floor   Mezzanine

Third floor   Forth floor

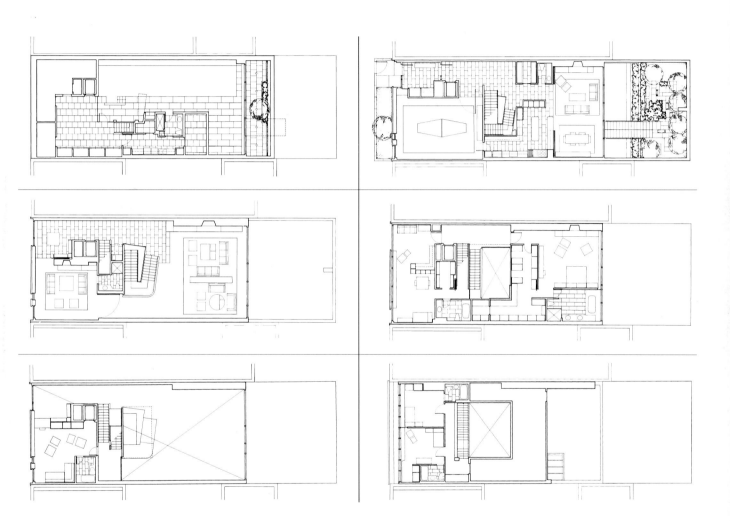

Transverse cross-section   Façade on the street

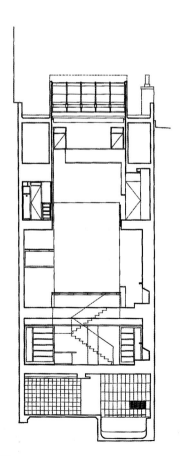

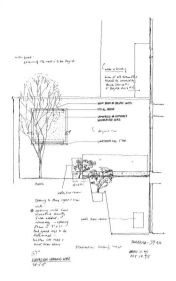

Study sketch   Longitudinal cross-section
for the garden

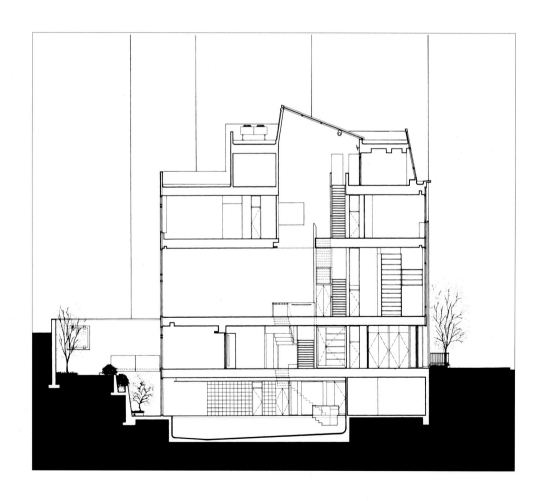

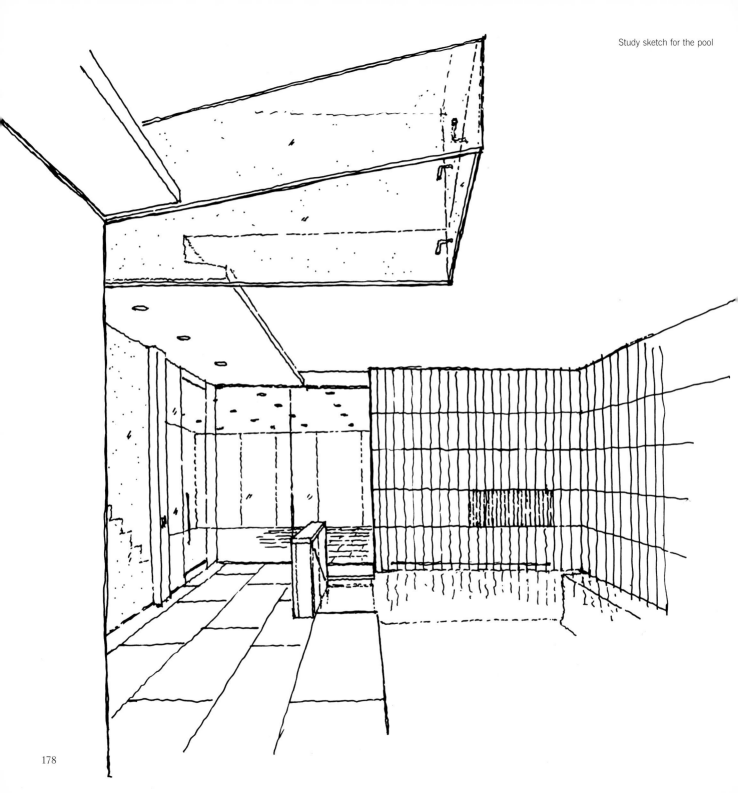

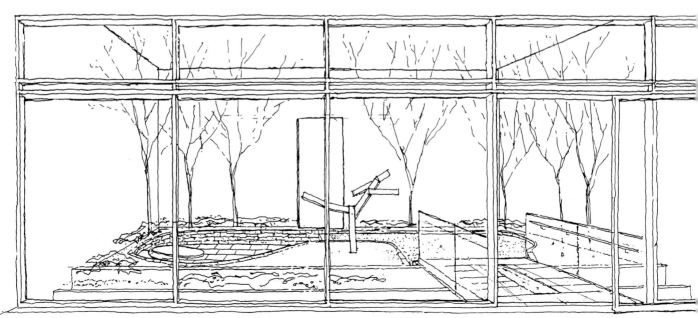

slightly enlarged
wall Buttress hides
small storage

Main drawing room
on the second floor

Detail of the stairwell

Detail of the handrail
of the main stairway,
preparatory sketch

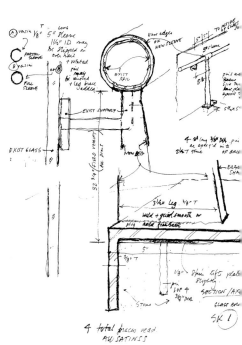

BRIDGE BRACES

Detail of the glass prism
of the main stairway

Detail of the main
stairway

Learning from…

Michael Sorkin,
Brooklyn waterfront,
Brooklyn, New York,
1993–94

'The Matrix is a computer-generated dream built to keep us under control'.[1]

In a dramatic encounter set in a dimension midway between dream and nightmare, Morpheus, leader and guide to the rebels, explains to Neo, predestined to free humanity from the slavery of the machines, the truth about the Matrix, the world in which we all apparently live and to which we are all slaves.

Two overlapping dimensions, one that commands and controls the other, humans reduced to living in a fictitious world because a glimpse of the truth would be intolerable: machines as the master of the world, and humanity exploited as a mere source of power.

Liberation takes place, of course, through a process of initiation that sees a chosen hero recognizing the truth (the real world is a single neuronal informational artifact that envelops us) and then leading rebellious humanity toward victory.

The Matrix is certainly the most sophisticated film produced in a larger school of movies dedicated to the Internet and the Web during the Nineties. A film that is at once a view of the world as an alchemistical process and view of the dark side of our problematic relationship with machinery, virtual reality, and a progressive distancing from the tactile and material dimension on the part of humanity at large.

The impetuous entry of the Internet and virtual reality into contemporary society is only the last step in a problematic relationship with an idea of modernity in a continual state of metamorphosis and with its capacity to influence our perception of time, our view, and the environment in which we live.

At the same time there is an increasingly powerful overlapping between real territory, subject to a significant mutation in the last decade, and the networks of computer systems that are colonizing and shaping the entire country in accordance with a social and economic demand for information.

The impact of the use of information technology and especially of the Internet on everyday living, on the spaces that we inhabit and work in, and on the successive reorganization of the community spaces seems to weigh increasingly heavily on the image that the city and surrounding territory will have over the coming decades.[2]

Reality seems to disappear under the weight of an ungovernable and indescribable complexity with the traditional tools of analysis of the territory and its economic, social, and physical structure.

The incredible urban visions, the zoomorphic grafts of mutant bodies on the interior of the chaotic urban fabric produced from the beginning of the Nineties on by Lebeus Woods and Michael Sorkin seem to materialize the dreams and at the same time the nightmares of an elite that is still too distant from the cities and their violent contradictions.

And the official architectural culture, one of the natural points of reference in the relationship between society and the built form, responds with a difficulty that is now evident, showing attitudes that fluctuate between the construction of unprecedented, spectacular forms, and the growing awareness of a progressive dematerialization of the built form on the interior of the contemporary city.

Both design attitudes clearly reveal in any case a state of crisis that involves both the operative and cultural instruments of architecture and the social role of the architect, who, beginning from the second half of the Sixties, was involved in the generalized disillusionment in professionalism understood as a warranty in the social administration of modernity.[3]

The American architectural culture of the last decade can offer a significant cross-section of these dynamics. And the reasons that make this reality so significant can be identified in a series of elements intertwined one with another: as a dimension in which the relationship between modernization, social acceptance and elaboration of the means of communication have been particularly radical and advanced; as a reality in which the academic cultural elaboration still exerts a considerable influence within certain political and economic elites; as a design and productive dimension in which the relationship between new technologies and traditional tools was left especially open to discussion, and, finally, as an intellectual milieu that, beginning from the early Sixties, was able to carry on a series of theoretical and programmatic elaborations capable of reflecting on the epistemological condition of doing architecture.

It would in fact be reductive to think of *Blob architecture*, the most fashionable linguistic trend of the moment, or the recent designs by Peter Eisenman and Frank Gehry as an autonomous expression, produced only by an 'artistic' and individual relationship with the project.[4] I believe, instead, that it is much more important to emphasize the capacity, which formed an important part of American architectural culture, to reflect on oneself and on the reasoning behind contemporary design, thus engendering some of the most important intellectual and creative experiences of the end of the twentieth century.

One of the most significant roots of this recent phase were certainly the writings[5] of Robert Venturi and Denise Scott Brown which especially appeared at the end of the Sixties,[6] a context of confrontation or radical opposition on the part of the international architectural culture, a turning point in the debate about modernity that had progressively developed since the end of the Second World War.[7]

Beginning with this phase we see the outlines of two tendencies which, counterpoised in a difficult dialogue, were decisively to influence American architecture and the very debate going on inside the universities: on the one hand, the populist tendency inaugurated by Venturi and Scott Brown which introduced the concept of the progressive disappearance of architecture on the interior of a generic city, and on the other hand, the reaction to the crisis through a formal response, internal to architecture, which returns to the roots of the Modern Movement, begun by the New York Five[8] and by the magazine *Oppositions*[9] in the early Seventies.

Corresponding to the different design and linguistic responses was, at the same time, a continuous questioning concerning the tools

Lebeus Woods,
Havana project,
La Habana, Cuba, 1995

of design and communication of architecture, clearly speaking to a problematic relationship with a social and material reality undergoing continual change. The social understanding of architecture remains basically a problem that characterized modern culture for the entire length of the twentieth century, and the garish pop of Venturi or the elitist, refined closure of a certain modernism both skirt this problem and, increasingly, the metropolitan condition as an inescapable background for design.

Surrounding these problematic cores, the situation of the last twenty years has considerable developed and become enriched with a debate that proposed 'critical regionalism' as a form of analysis capable of recovering the heterodox experiences from the provinces of the Empire and a commercial drift of the 'postmodern' taken hostage by Disney as 'corporate image'. And in the background there remains in any case the progressive loss of ethical and political value as an element of comparison in the design of architecture for a persistent attention to the object rather than its social influence.

On the interior of a debate that increasingly focused on formal and linguistich questions, the opposed experiences of Peter Eisenman[10] and Robert Venturi[11] were among the few capable of binding, often with evident ideological contrivances, the designed form and the theoretical elaboration.

Venturi continued undaunted in a series of variations on the theme in the relationship between architecture and social communication, in the quest for an architecture capable of losing itself in the city and, at the same time, to signify the city.

While the approach and progress of Eisenman is more complex, a virtual divining rod in the identification of signs and elements capable to binding more and more design with the deep structures of the territory and at the same time one of the more active, contradictory, and interesting 'agitprops' on the American scene.

One significant example is the construction beginning in 1990 of the circuit 'ANY' conferences[12] and the magazine of the same name, which viewed Eisenman as one of the more active operators. An extraordinary example of a network of exchanges and nomadic encounters on a global scale and certainly one of the most important intellectual workshops for the American scene of the Nineties, with the participation of Arata

Isozaki, Ignasi de Sola Morales, Rem Koolhaas, Frank Gehry, Daniel Libeskind, Rafael Moneo, Bernard Tschumi, and Jacques Derrida, but also young talents, such as Greg Lynn, Sanford Qwinter, Beatriz Colomina, Anthony Vidler, and Elizabeth Diller.

The globalized dimension in terms of exchanges and confrontations is reflected in the American universities with the arrival of several of the most interesting protagonists on the international scene.

The presence from the end of the Eighties on of, among others, Rem Koolhaas and Rafael Moneo at the Harvard Graduate School of Design (GSD), Bernard Tschumi at Columbia University, along with the policy of invitations and seminars undertaken intensely by MIT, SCI-Arc, Princeton, and Cooper Union enriched the quality of the debate and of the contributions by establishing once again a central role for American universities in the international debate.

The American debut of several of the protagonists consecrated by the exhibition at MoMA on Deconstructivism, grafted onto a growing theoretical and design structure, provoked at a distance, more than an increase of the adepts of the new language, an increase in speculation concerning the role of contemporary architecture and especially the relationship between representation, the applicacion of new technologies, and the form of design.

One direct consequence of this were the experiences of Greg Lynn,[13] Asymptote, Karl Chu and Kolatan/MacDonald studio,[14] which is to say, several of the American proponents of so-called *Blob architecture*, an expression of a generational change that took place in the second half of the Nineties and, at the same time, a language that expressed one of the possible responses to the delicate relationship between architecture, communications, virtuality, and the New Economy.

We are not talking about, as has often been suggested ironically, refined designers of web pages, but rather the emergence of a different dimension of doing architecture in the face of a social and economic demand subject to a powerful metamorphosis. The design for the Virtual Guggenheim by Asymptote or else the habitat organisms of the Embryologic Houses by Greg Lynn express the first uncertain steps of a discipline that looks to its own refoundation through the reform of the tools of design and representation, and a reflection on the relationship between man and virtual-

ANY, no. 0, 1993

Greg Lynn, Embryologic
Houses, 1998

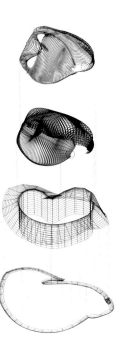

ity. The true risk in this phase lies rather in a self-referential formal dimension that forgets about the real city, taking refuge in an Eden of perfect and unattainable forms. We often find ourselves faced with works that are more concerned with the spectacular and media-driven effect, aware of an inevitable, rapid perishability in which the relationship between built form and applied construction technology still appears quite weak, as if the separation between shell/skin and structure was a question to be ignored.

Different and, from certain points of view, more mature is the work by Diller+Scofidio[15] which, through the design of temporary installations, have tried to develop a more active and participatory relationship between the user, the space involved, and the experimental use of new technologies and materials. By attempting to provoke the involuntary spectator to look beyond reality, to focus a less hasty attention. the installations of Diller+Scofidio construct an interface between the world of architecture, which attempts to understand change, seeking the tools to do so in other disciplines as well, and a metropolitan reality rich in stimuli and a perennial source of teaching and learning.

[1] *The Matrix*, directed by the Wachowski Brothers, 140', USA 1999.
[2] Impacts on the territory are already partially visible, ranging from the flight from the agrarian regions of the Midwest toward the big cities (see Peter T. Kilborn, 'Boom in Economy Skips Towns on the Plains', in *The New York Times*, 2 July 2000) right up to several recent studies on the impact of the Internet on the city: William J. Mitchell, *E.topia*, Cambridge (Mass.), MIT Press, 1999; Jeremy Rifkin, *The Age of Access*, New York 2000; 'High-Fiber Diet, Growth of US Optical Networks', in *Wired*, June 2000, pp. 142–46.
[3] See Donald A. Schon, *The Reflective Practitioner*, Basic Books, 1983; Donald A. Schon, Martin Rein, *Frame Reflection*, Basic Books, 1994.
[4] The ideas of Greg Lynn and Hani Rashid, cofounder of Asymptote with Lise Anne Couture, and considered among the most significant creators of *Blob architecture* were the basis of the American Pavilion at the recent International Biennial of Architecture (2000) with a work in progress with students from UCLA. Similarly, the works of Frank Gehry and Peter Eisenman opened the Nineties and were representatives of American architecture in the previous edition in Venice in 1991.
[5] Robert Venturi, *Complexity and Contradiction in Architecture*, New York, Museum of Modern Art, 1966; Denise Scott Brown, Robert Venturi, 'A Significance for A&P Parking Lots, or Learning from Las Vegas', in *Architectural Forum*, March 1968, pp. 37–43, 89–91; Denise Scott Brown, Robert Venturi, *Learning from Las Vegas*, Cambridge (Mass.), MIT Press, 1972.
[6] 'Robert Venturi (…) introduced the act of reflection of architecture upon itself', in Alexander Tzonis, Liane Lefaivre, Richard Diamond, *Architecture in North America since 1960*, London, Thames and Hudson, 1995, pp. 32 and following.
[7] I am referring primarily to the debate on the Modern Movement in England and the polemical interventions of Rayner Banham, James Stirling, and the Smithsons.
[8] Robert Stern, *Five Architects*, New York, Wittenborn, 1973; Manfredo Tafuri, *Five Architects N.Y.*, Rome, Officina Edizioni, 1981; Alexander Tzonis, Liane Lefaivre, Richard Diamond, *op. cit.*, pp. 38–44.
[9] See Michael K. Hays (edited by), *Oppositions Reader*, New York, Princeton Architectural Press, 1998.
[10] Peter Eisenman, *Diagram Diaries*, New York, Universe, 1999.
[11] Robert Venturi, *Iconography and Electronics upon a Generic Architecture*, Cambridge (Mass.), MIT Press, 1996.
[12] Cynthia Davidson (edited by), 'ANY (story)', in *Lotus*, no. 92, March 1996, pp. 94–131 and, in the same issue, an article by Mirko Zardini, 'La sigla è la strategia', pp. 114–15.
[13] Greg Lynn, *Folds, Bodies and Blobs*, Brussels, La Lettre Volée, 1998.
[14] See among the various contributions, the latest issues of the journal *ANY*, to which Greg Lynn contributed extensively, issue 65 of *Architectural Design* (May-June 1998), and issue 822 of *Domus* (January 2000).
[15] Elizabeth Diller, Riccardo Scofidio, *Flesh*, New York, Princeton Architectural Press, 1994; Aaron Betsky, 'Under Surveillance', in *Architecture*, June 2000, pp. 128–47.

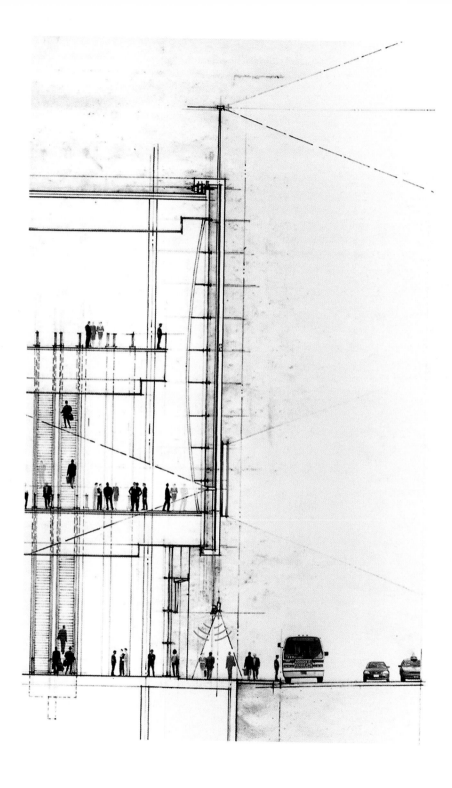

Seattle Art Museum, Seattle, Washington, 1984–91

Venturi, Scott Brown and Associates
In association with: Olson/Sundberg Arch.

This design for a new Art Museum in Seattle, carried on in parallel with the expansion of the National Gallery of London (1986–91), appears as a concrete response to the debate underway in the Eighties and Nineties on the 'new' forms of art museums.

As with most of the projects by Robert Venturi and Denise Scott Brown, spatial choices, the use of decoration, and theoretical vision intersect in an effort to charge the built form with a communicative quality capable of establishing a new bond with society and its complexities.

And in this subtle polemic with the contemporary affirmation of an 'expressionist and visionary' approach to the design of a museum, Venturi counterbalanced a logic that favored the traditional view of the museum as a 'generic loft', a flexible and non-invasive space capable of accommodating a demand that is complex and heterogeneous, in exhibition and social terms.

The museum, in the intentions of the client, is meant in fact to accommodate a flexible number of events and activities linked to the city's community, to host workshops, teaching and informative spaces, the administrative structure and at the same time must house a major collection of Asian, African, and native American art.

The project is located in the downtown area of Seattle, a portion of city organized by a rigid street grid with a use predominantly given to commerce, service industry, and middle-class residential zones.

The building fits into the context by offering a series of interesting formal and locational solutions which aim to reinforce the museum's public, civic, and friendly role in the city.

The two main entrances are located on the two 'lesser' fronts which overlook First and Second Avenues, two roads that run parallel at two differentiated elevations that are reconciled by a long stairway that runs along the main side.

The entrance on First Avenue corresponds to the semicircular treatment of the façade, which contradicts the urban grid by creating an alluring invitation to a visitor, with the counterpoint of the large sculpture *Hammering Man* by Jonathan Borofsky.

All of the fronts of the museum are conceived as a continuous dialogue between large and small scales, in which the decorative solution of the portal and their syncopated sequence, plays with the etching in large letters of the name of the museum and the fluting and grooves of the stone facing, while the exterior stairway is mirrored in the large interior staircase in the museum which leads from the lower lobby to the exhibition halls.

The need of artificially lighting all of the spaces in the museum, and therefore of having the museum as a large box, closed to the exterior, convinced Venturi and Scott Brown to emphasize the external decorative dimension of the building and to seek links with the city.

The main stair becomes, as in the project for the National Gallery in London and in the Children's Museum of Houston (1989–92), a crucial element of the design, in which the museum is mirrored in the city and vice versa, while the sequence of exhibition halls on the two upper floors follows a classical and non-invasive design of the relationship between artworks and the visitor.

Overall view
of the museum

The museum and the city

Study sketch

Entrance to the museum
and the sculpture
Hammering Man
by Jonathan Borofsky

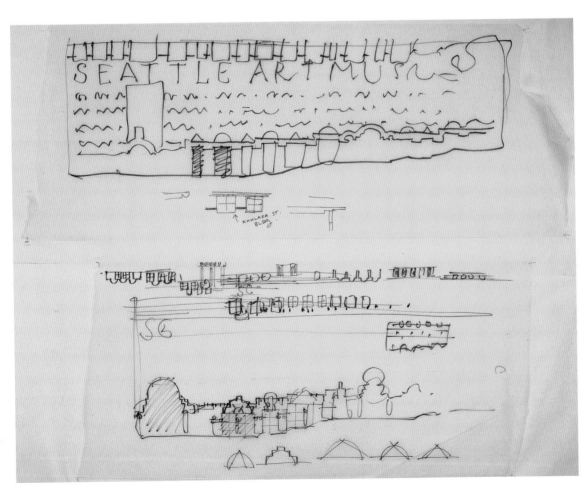

Longitudinal cross-section

Elevation on University
Street

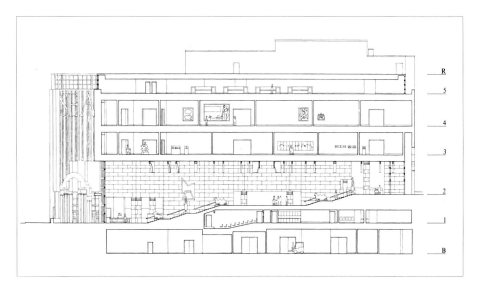

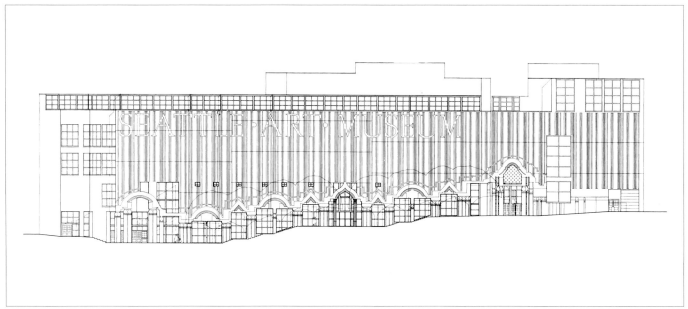

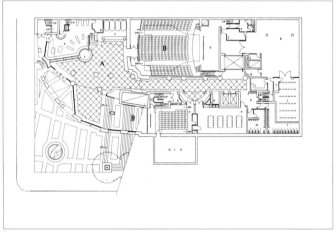

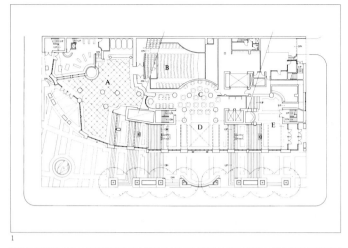

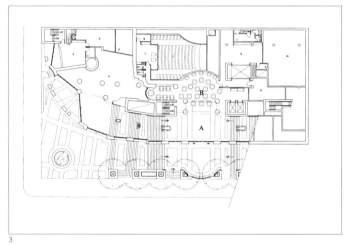

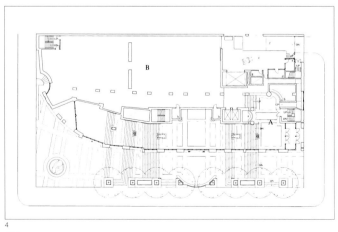

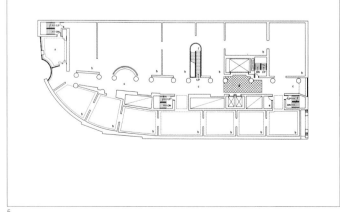

1. Ground floor   Entrance

2. Second floor

3. Mezzanine

4. Third floor

5. Fourth floor

Main stairway giving
access to the museum
spaces

Axonometric projection
in cross-section

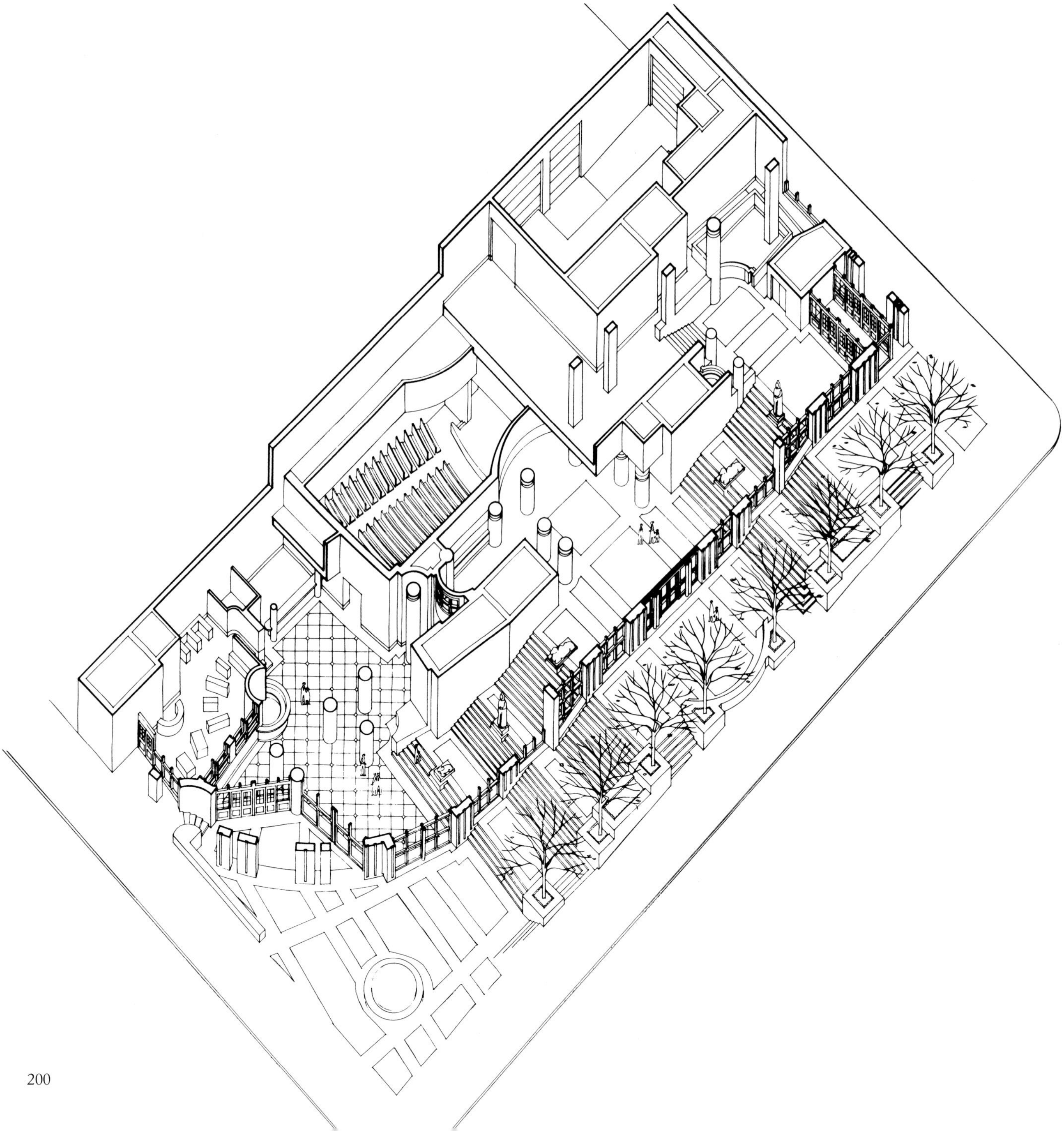

Frederick R. Weisman Museum, Minneapolis, Minnesota, 1990–93

Frank O. Gehry
Project principal: R. Hale
Collaborators: V. Jenkins, M. Fineout, E. Chan

'We decided to use a brilliant finish on the Weisman Museum because of the light of Minneapolis: in the end I realized it would work' (Frank Gehry).

At the beginning of the Nineties, Gehry worked on three different museum projects that established a scale of fundamental temporal and conceptual progression for the Canadian architect and for his critical reception: the Toledo Museum of Art, the Frederick R. Weisman Museum in Minneapolis, and the first phase Guggenheim Museum in Bilbao.

This is a sequence that narrates the progressive revelation of a material solution that was at the same time a poetic intuition: a passage that accompanied the research into movement applied to the body of the architecture and which progressively marked the projects by Gehry over the last two decades.

Thus, the Toledo Museum, with a sculptural composition that recalls the assembly of the volumes of the Schnabel House, seems to conclude a first phase begun a few years before with the European projects for Vitra, in which the use of lead-coated copper as a covering for the various structural bodies allowed a foreshadowing of a research in progress on the complex relationship between structure and skin.

The abandonment of the heavy lead-coated copper for sheets of galvanized steel demonstrates a fundamental passage that would find its definitive affirmation and formal application in the Bilbao Guggenheim. It is as if air can finally pass through the interstitial passages that now separate the remarkable skeleton of the architecture from its fragile skin.

A passage that sends a shiver that shakes the entire building ever so slightly, showing its fragility as well as its gleaming beauty.

At the same time, the Weisman Museum displays that delicate passion for contextualization that Gehry applies in some cases to his creations, in search of a visual and material relationship among the various faces of the building and the context surrounding it.

In this case, the museum, set on the edges of the campus of the University of Minnesota and on the banks of the Mississippi River, finds itself obliged to play a two-fold urban and territorial role as a hinge between city and university and at the same time as the campus's frontage on the river.

The choice of materials for the covering, therefore, hearkens back also to the location of the museum, making use of stainless steel for the façade that is reflected in the river and brick, instead, for the sides that look back toward the more traditional university compound.

The new structure is composed of four storeys above ground set against a light incline that overlooks the river, which Gehry skilfully used to create on the second floor a technical sector and a covered parking area (capacity for one hundred and twenty cars).

The third floor is likewise used for more technical rooms, the museum's warehousing, and access ramps to the parking areas, linking the museum directly with one of the main arteries near the campus, while pedestrian access is ensured by a walkway that leads to the main floor and the lobby.

It is on the fourth floor that we find the most representative spaces, with the galleries that house the Weisman Collection, lit by a system of skylights treated in a sculptural manner, channeling natural light to the interior of the museum. At the centre of the fourth floor, on the other hand, there is a 1,500-square-foot auditorium designed for audio and video performances, organized with a system of movable panels and linked to the lobby that overlooks the Mississippi River.

The top floor of the museum is destined for administrative use and executive offices, organized around the highest point on the river front.

Study sketch

General view of the north side of the museum

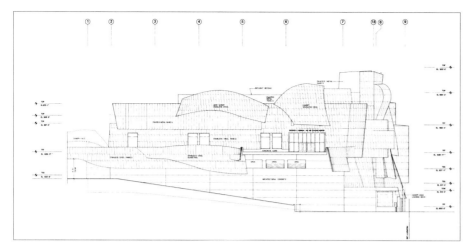

South elevation

Longitudinal cross-section
from south to north

North elevation

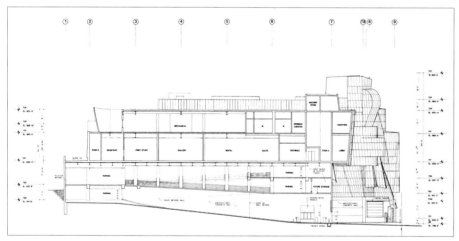

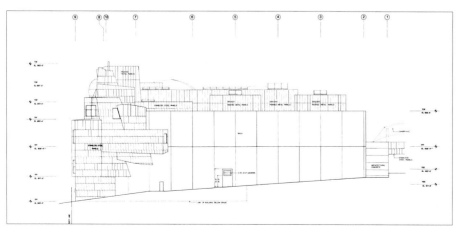

The museum and
the surrounding space

Detail of the external
facing

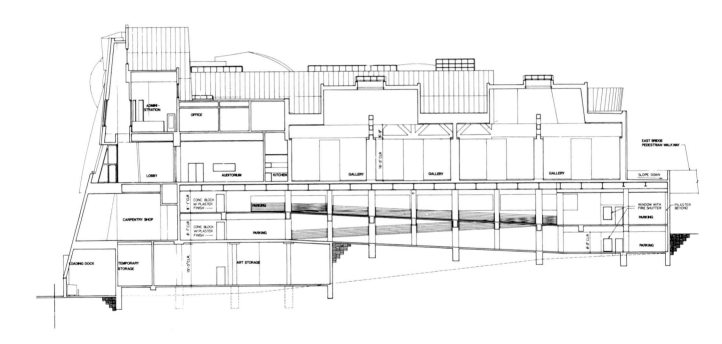

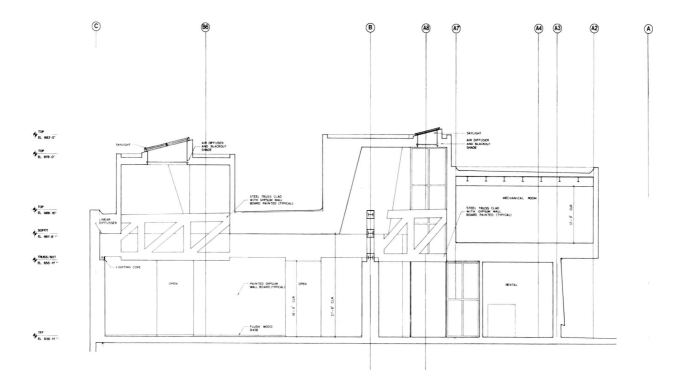

The beam of the skylight

Interior of the gallery

Aronoff Center for Design and Art, Cincinnati, Ohio, 1986–96

Peter Eisenman
Collaborators: G. Kewin, R. Rosson, D. Barry,
G. Lynn, M. McInturf, J. Walters

One of the most complex and elaborate projects in the creative experience of Peter Eisenman, the Aronoff Center is part of a larger overall project for the reform of the campus of the Cincinnati University which called for other works by Frank Gehry, Michael Graves, Pei, Cobb, Freed & Partners, and Venturi and Scott Brown.

The building, with a total surface area of 25,000 square metres, distributed over the restructuring of the existing works and the new intervention, is destined to house 2,000 persons, including students and researchers, thus constituting the core of the College of Design, Architecture, and Planning, for a total investment of 35 million dollars.

The project stands as one of the first designs executed on an urban scale by Eisenman, just subsequent to the designs of the Wexner Center at Ohio University (1983–89) and the Iba Checkpoint Charlie Residence in Berlin (1981–85), and in close continuity with a larger reflection that creates a relationship between a complex application of diagram, as a design tool, and the context (site).

In this case, the intervention is prompted by the reorganization and expansion of the existing university site, a large zigzag building dating from the Sixties, which, along with the level curves of the adjoining land, immediately becomes one of the texts upon which the New York architect intervenes, taking from it series of basic rules for the new project.

This is not a mechanical and deductive operation; rather it is an attempt to make a problematic approach to a context that no longer has any basic rules upon which to rely.

The building thus becomes a tool of theoretical reflection, the concrete manifestation of a work in progress, a body animated by a perpetual motion and, at the same time, a direct experience by the art and architecture students of the complexity and density of reality.

In the expansion project, Eisenman works on a dual cognitive and design system that, by merging, generates the final structure: the silhouette of the existing building, whose broken line is redeveloped to the point of giving form to a new aggregate space, and the level lines of the land, from which emerges a curve conceived as a 'curve without centre', that is, as an infinitely segmented line and not as a derivation of an existing circle.

The creative and compositional process follows the principle of 'symmetry breaking', i.e., an attempt to visualize a complexity through non-linear logic, and the result is a building that in the intentions of the designer, was meant to 'change reality instead of reflecting it'.

The addition, powerfully integrated with the existing works, is organized on three stacked levels that fit together so as to multiply the spaces for meeting, interacting, transparency, communication, and discovery.

An interior street and a system of ramps, punctuated by the natural lighting of the skylights and by a refined design in neon, thus link the auditorium, the library, the workshops, the classrooms, and the cafeterias, thus introducing into the building the complexity of an urban experience that is quite distant from the arcadian atmosphere of so many university campuses.

On the exterior, the Aronoff Center immediately reveals all of the conceptual violence with which the design is charged through a complex design of floors, with jutting elements and apertures that is reinforced by the application of eleven different colours and facings capable of further reinforcing this perception.

General model

Entrance to the north-east

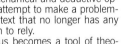
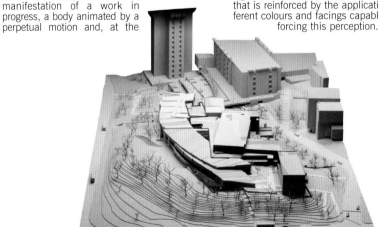

U.C.D.A.A.P.
Concept Diagrams

Curved Line

Chevrons

Segmented Line

Alms   D.A.A.   Wolfson

Existing Building

Exponenial Overlaps (1.6)

Asymptotic Tilts (1.2)

Ideal Chevron

Vertical Stepping

Exponential Torque (1.1)

Trace of Existing Building Aligned with Wolfson

Phase Shift

Trace of Existing Building Aligned with Alms

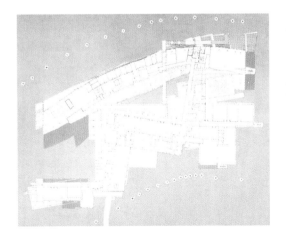

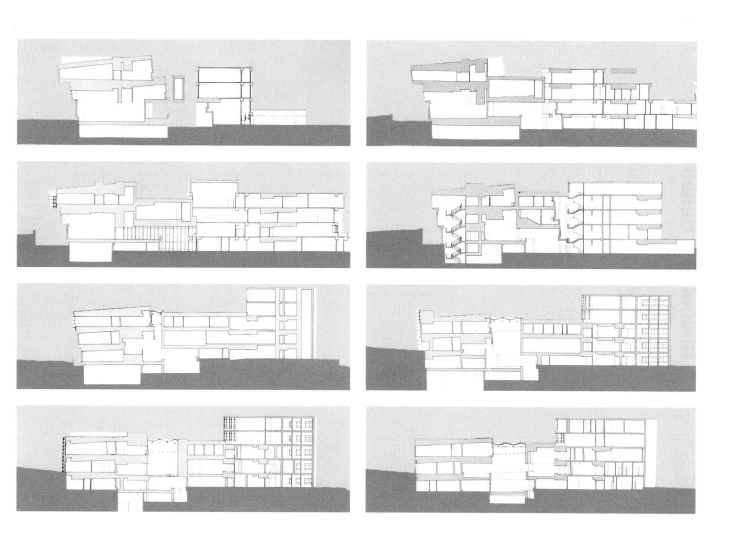

Façade to the north

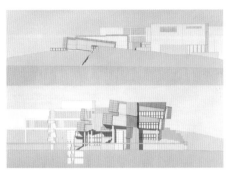

Detail of the façade
to the north

Hallway leading to the
library and stairway
leading to the third floor

The auditorium

Interior spaces
on the third floor

Interior Expansion of the New York Stock Exchange, 1997–99

Asymptote
Lise Anne Couture and Hani Rashid
with E. Didyk, J. Cleater

The advanced operations centre of the New York Stock Exchange and the design of its computer derivation represent an interesting example of a new service architecture in which virtual and real spaces are perfectly integrated and assimilated.

In this case, in fact, the commission called for an intervention on the interior of the second floor of the Stock Exchange building, in a narrow space, a passageway between the main trading room and the Blue Room, a subsequent expansion in which to visualize the complexity and vastness of the trades underway, and at the same to reconfigure a virtual space that might allow both traders and investors a greater potentiality for understanding and intervention on the various financial marketplaces.

The main area of the two projects is the continuous flow of data and the objective was the real-time perception of the changes, the possibility of finding ease of orientation and attaining simplicity of intervention.

A space perfectly in keeping with the principles of the New Economy that are serving as a flywheel to the American economy of the last decade, overturning the traditional laws of financial life and imposing an increasingly rapid relationship between time and effects.

The heart of the project is the application of the 3DTFV (Three Dimensional Trading Floor) computer system, a three-dimensional visualization system for the information and data that are continually transmitted in several of the sixty ultra-flat liquid-crystal monitors mounted along the two walls that make up this new space, the interior nerve centre of the Stock Exchange.

The design of the real space is conceived as a theatrical presentation capable of astonishing and arousing curiosity in those who approach.

The area, narrow, a passageway between the two large trading rooms, is in fact treated through the covering of the walls with an undulating surface in rear-lighted light-blue glass in which are mounted the videos that make up the wall of financial data information.

The space is conceived as a sort of modern cave of marvels, a unit capable summoning the visitor and capturing his or her interest.

A circular sculptural element is inserted into the metal-lined ceiling, and in it an LED chart indicates the current stock quotes, while the floor is treated in coloured epoxy resin with steel inserts tumbling out toward the adjoining rooms.

At the same time Asymptote designed and built a virtual space that simulates the space of the stock exchange, allowing traders and mere visitors to orient themselves and obtain as much available information to navigate and operate in the Stock Exchange.

The virtual environment developed in 3DTFV is a veritable digital landscape, navigable and interactive, conceived as an architectural space in which to easily obtain the information and variables produced in trading. The variable topography of the 'hot floor' expands and changes colour in accordance with the changes in the various financial areas, generating visual stimuli that are easily interpreted by the user.

The two dimensions, real and virtual, were conceived as mirroring each other, capable of being integrated and indicating reciprocal emotional and information potentials.

General view of the new expansion

WELCOME YOU TO THE VIRTUAL VORTEX THE NEW YORK

The metal-lined ceiling
and the LED chart
indicating the current
stock quotes

Detail of the main board

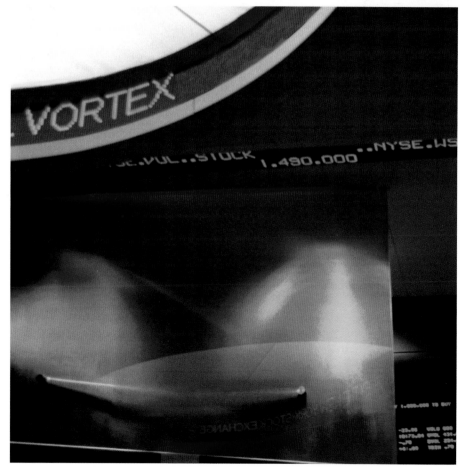

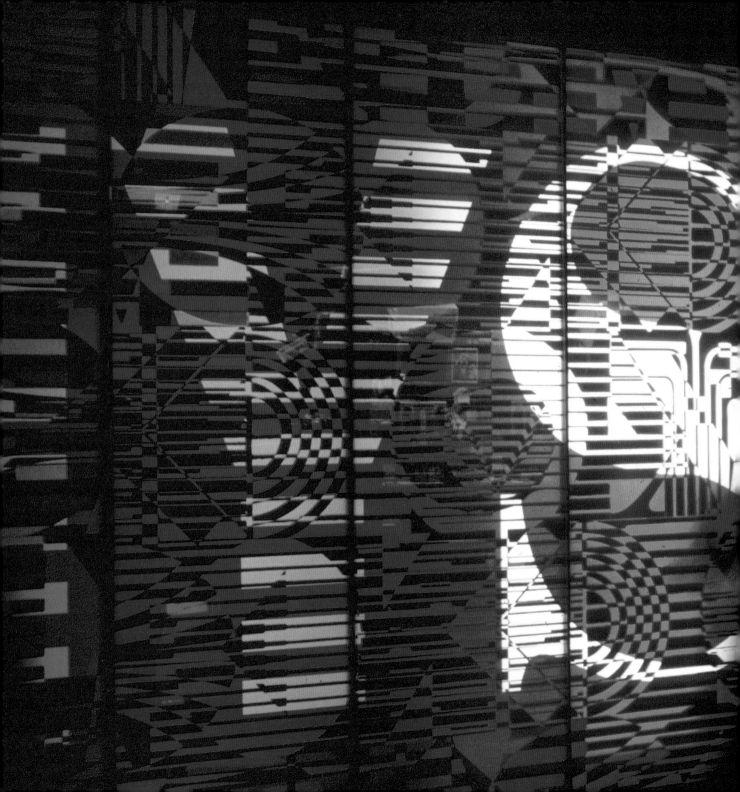

Detail of the main wall
in the interior expansion

Detail of the flow of stock
prices

General view
of the virtual environment

The flow of stock prices
visualized on the interior
of the new virtual space

Appendix

edited by Chiara Geracà and Luca Molinari

Biographies

Asymptote

561 Broadway 5A, New
York, New York 10012
Phone 212 343 7333
Fax 212 343 7099
E-mail
info@asymptote.net /
www.asymptote.com

The studio of Asymptote
was founded in 1988 by
Lise Anne Couture and
Hani Rashid.
Lise Anne Couture was
born in Montreal, Canada
and took a degree in
Architecture at Yale
University in 1986.
Hani Rashid was born
in Cairo, Egypt, and took
a degree in Architecture
at the Academy of Art
at Cranbrook in 1985.
Both architects have been
teaching at the university
level since the late
Eighties.
Lise Anne Couture has
taught, among other
places, at: Berlage
Institute, Amsterdam;
Graduate School of
Design (GSD), Harvard
University; Columbia
University Graduate
School of Architecture,
Planning and
Preservation, New York;
Parsons School of Design,
New York.
Hani Rashid has taught,
on the other hand, at:

Royal Danish Academy,
Copenhagen; Southern
California Institute of
Architecture (SCI-Arc),
Los Angeles; Graduate
School of Design at
Harvard University;
Columbia University
Graduate School of
Architecture, Planning
and Preservation,
New York.

Selected Projects
2000
Mission Armory Center,
San Francisco, California;
Offices of the
Guggenheim,
New York, New York
1999
Guggenheim Center
for Art and Technology,
New York, New York;
New York Stock
Exchange, Advanced
Trading Floor Operations
Center, New York,
New York;
Guggenheim Virtual
Museum, New York,
New York
1998
Music Theatre
(competition), Graz,
Austria;
New York Stock
Exchange Virtual Trading
Floor (3DTFV), Second
phase, New York,
New York
1997
LegoZone Display Area,

Billund, Denmark;
New York Stock
Exchange Virtual Trading
Floor (3DTFV), First
phase, New York,
New York
1996
Univers Multimedia
Theatre, Aarhus, Denmark
1995
National Museum
of Korea (competition),
Seoul, Korea
1993
Contemporary Arts
Center (competition),
Tours, France
1992
Times Square (design),
New York, New York
1991
National Dutch Court
House (competition),
Groningen, Holland
1990
Moscow State Theatre
(competition), Moscow,
Russia
1989
Library of Alexandria
(competition),
Alexandria, Egypt;
West Coast Gateway
Monument, Los Angeles,
California

William P. Bruder

1314 West Circle
Mountain Road,
New River, Arizona 85087
Phone 602 465 7399
Fax 602 465 0109
E-mail
bruder@netwest.com /
www.willbruder.com

Will Bruder was born
in Milwaukee, Wisconsin,
in 1946. He took
a degree in Sculpture
at the University of
Wisconsin-Milwaukee and
a post-graduate degree in
Architecture at the same
university, in 1974. In the
first half of the Sixties he
collaborated with Paolo
Soleri in the first
community of Arcosanti,
in Arizona.
He founded the studio
of William P. Bruder –
Architect in 1974 in
New River, Arizona.
He has taught at:
Massachusetts Institute
of Technology (MIT),
SCI-Arc, Yale University,
and Georgia Tech.

Selected Projects
2000
New School for the Arts,
Tempe, Arizona;
Kursh Residence, Marin
County, California
1999
Nevada Museum of Art,

Reno, Nevada;
Scottsdale Museum
of Contemporary Art,
Scottsdale, Arizona
1995–97
Mad River Boat Trips,
Jackson, Wyoming
1992–94
Deer Valley Rock Art
Center, Phoenix, Arizona;
Temple Kol Ami,
Scottsdale, Arizona
1989–95
Central Library, Phoenix,
Arizona

Peter Eisenman

41 West 25th Street,
New York, New York
10010
Phone 212 645 1400
Fax 212 645 0725
E-mail earch@idt.net /
www.petereisenman.com

Peter Eisenman was born
in New York in 1932.
He took a degree
in Architecture at Cornell
University, a post-graduate
degree at Columbia
University, and a doctorate
at Cambridge University,
in England.
Peter Eisenman has taught
at the universities of
Cambridge, Princeton,
Yale, Harvard, at the
University of Illinois,
and at Ohio State
University. He founded
the studio of Eisenman
Architects in 1980
in New York.
He has written and
published many works
on architecture, including
House X (Rizzoli, 1982),
Fin d'Ou T HouS (The
Architectural Association,
1986), *Houses of Cards*
(Oxford University
Press, 1987), *Diagram
Diaries* (Universe, 1999),
Chora L Works with
Jacques Derrida
(Monacelli Press, 1997),
and *Giuseppe Terragni:*
Transformations,
Decompositions, Critiques
(Monacelli Press, 2000).

Selected Projects
1998
Arizona Cardinals
Stadium, Mesa, Arizona
1998–2001
Holocaust Monument,
Berlin, Germany
1997
Staten Island Institute
of Arts and Sciences,
New York, New York
1996
BFL Software, Corporate
Headquarters, Bangalore,
India
1992
Max Reinhardt Haus
(project), Berlin,
Germany
1989–93
Greater Columbus
Convention Center,
Columbus, Ohio
1988–90
Koizumi Sangyo Building,
Tokyo, Japan
1986–96
Aronoff Center for Design
and Art, Cincinnati
University, Cincinnati,
Ohio
1983–89
Wexner Center for Visual
Arts, State University,
Columbus, Ohio
1981–85
Iba Checkpoint Charlie
Residence, Berlin,
Germany

1972–75
House VI, Cornwall,
Connecticut
1969–70
House II, Hardwick,
Vermont
1967–68
House I, Princeton, New
Jersey

Frank O. Gehry

1520-B Cloverfield
Boulevard, Santa Monica,
California 90404
Phone 310 828 6088
Fax 310 828 2098

Frank Gehry was born
in Toronto, Canada,
in 1929.
He took a degree
in Architecture in 1954
at the University
of Southern California
and he studied Urban
Planning at the Graduate
School of Design at
Harvard University.
Before opening his own
studio, Gehry worked
with Victor Gruen
(1953–54, 1958–61),
Robert and Company
(1955–56), Hideo Sasaki
(1957), William Pereira
(1957–58), and André
Remondet (1961).
Eventually he founded
the studio of Frank
O. Gehry & Associates
in 1962 in Santa Monica,
California.
In 1982, 1985, and from
1987 to 1989, Frank
Gehry held the 'Charlotte
Davenport' Chair
of Architecture
at Yale University.
In 1984 he was awarded
the 'Eliot Noyes' Chair
at Harvard University
GSD.

Selected Projects
1998
Porta di Venezia, Venice,
Italy
1998
Stata Complex, MIT,
Cambridge, Massachusetts
1995–2000
Experience Music Project,
Seattle, Washington
1995–99
DG Bank, Berlin,
Germany
1994–99
Der neue Zollhof,
Düsseldorf, Germany
1994–96
Nationale-Nederlanden
Building, Prague, Czech
Republic
1991–97
Guggenheim Museum,
Bilbao, Spain
1990–93
Frederick R. Weisman
Museum, Minneapolis,
Minnesota
1990–92
Arts Building, University
of Toledo, Toledo, Ohio
1989–92
Entertainment Center,
Euro Disney,
Marne-la-Vallée, France
1988–93
American Center, Paris,
France
1987
Disney Concert Hall,
Los Angeles, California
1987–96
Team Disneyland,
Anaheim, California

1987–89
Vitra Museum, Weil
am Rhein, Germany
1986–89
Schnabel House,
Brentwood, California

Gwathmey, Siegel & Associates Architects

475 Tenth Avenue,
New York, New York
10018
Phone 212 947 1240
Fax 212 967 0890
www.gwathmey-siegel.com

The studio of Gwathmey,
Siegel & Associates
Architects was founded
by Charles Gwathmey
and Robert Siegel
in 1968, in New York.
Charles Gwathmey was
born in 1938 in Charlotte,
North Carolina.
He took a degree
in Architecture
in 1962 at Yale University.
From 1965 until 1991
he taught at the Pratt
Institute, UCLA,
Princeton University,
Columbia University,
the University of Texas,
and at the University
of California
at Los Angeles.
From 1983 to 1999
he taught at Yale
University and in 1985
he was awarded
the 'Eliot Noyes' Chair
at Harvard University.
Robert Siegel took
a degree in Architecture
in 1962 at Yale University
and a post-graduate
degree in 1963 at Harvard
University.

Selected Projects
1992
Solomon R. Guggenheim
Museum (addition),
New York, New York
1991
Conference Center, Disney
World, Orlando, Florida
1990
Busch-Reisinger / Fine
Arts Library
expansion of the Fogg
Art Museum, Cambridge,
Massachusetts
1988
American Museum
of the Moving Image,
Astoria, New York

Steven Holl

435 Hudson Street,
Suite 402, New York,
New York 10014
Phone 212 989 0918
Fax 212 463 9718
E-mail
mail@stevenholl.com /
www.stevenholl.com

Steven Holl was born
in 1947 in Bremerton,
Washington.
He took a degree
in Architecture at
Washington University
in 1971 and did
post-graduate studies
in 1976 at the
Architectural Association
(AA) in London.
The studio of Steven Holl
Architects was founded
by Steven Holl in New
York, in 1976.
Steven Holl has taught
since 1981 at Columbia
University as well as at
Washington University,
Syracuse University,
Pratt Institute, and
Parsons School of Design.
Among the publications
by Steven Holl we
should mention the two
Pamphlet Architecture:
no. 5 'The Alphabetical
City' (New York, 1980),
and no. 9 *Rural and
Urban House Types
in North America*
(New York, 1982).

Selected Projects
1999–2001
MIT Dormitories,
Cambridge, Massachusetts
1998–2000
Pavilion, Amsterdam,
Holland
1997–2000
Bellevue Art Museum,
Bellevue, Washington
1996–99
Cranbrook Institute
of Science, Bloomfield
Hills, Michigan
1994–97
Chapel of St Ignatius,
Seattle University,
Seattle, Washington
1993–98
Kiasma Museum of
Contemporary Art,
Helsinki, Finland
1992–97
Makuhari Residences,
Chiba, Japan
1989–92
Stretto House,
Dallas, Texas
1989–91
Void Space/Hinged
Space Residenz, Nexus
World Fukuoka, Japan
1988
AGB Library
(competition), Berlin,
Germany
1984–88
Hybrid Building,
Seaside, Florida

Machado and Silvetti & Associates

560 Harrison Avenue,
Boston, Massachusetts
02118
Phone 617 426 7070
Fax 617 426 3604
www.machado-silvetti.com

The studio of Machado
and Silvetti & Associates
was founded by Rodolfo
Machado and Jorge
Silvetti in Boston in 1985,
even though the two
architects had already
been working together
as associates since 1974.
Both are professors in the
Graduate School of
Design at Harvard
University.
Currently Rodolfo
Machado teaches Urban
Planning in the School
of Design at Harvard
University, while Jorge
Silvetti is the head of
the Department of
Architecture.

Selected Projects
2002
Villa Getty (restoration),
Malibu, California;
Student Residence,
Cambridge, Massachusetts
2001
Allston Branch of the
Boston Public Library,
Boston, Massachusetts;
Marcia and John Price

Museum Building, for the
Museum of Art, Salt Lake
City, Utah
1998
Plan for the Mission Bay
Campus, University
of California, San
Francisco, California;
Master Plan, Parking
and Scully Hall,
Princeton, New Jersey
1996
Robert F. Wagner Jr Park,
New York, New York
1995
Villa, Concord,
Massachusetts

Richard Meier

475 Tenth Avenue,
New York,
New York 10018
Phone 212 967 6060
Fax 212 967 3207

Richard Meier was born
in 1934 in Newark,
New Jersey.
He took a degree in
Architecture in 1957
at Cornell University
and has worked at the
Studio SOM and with
Marcel Breuer.
He founded the studio
of Richard Meier
& Partners in 1963
in New York.
He has taught in many
schools of Architecture,
including the Cooper
Union, Pratt Institute,
Yale University, the GSD
of Harvard, and UCLA.
He won the Pritzker Prize
in 1984.

Selected Projects
1996
Museum of the Ara Pacis,
Rome, Italy
1996–2001
Church of the Year 2000,
Rome, Italy
1995–2000
Federal Buildings
and U.S. Courthouse,
Phoenix, Arizona
1994–96
Museum of Television and
Radio, Beverly Hills,
California
1991–94
Swiss Air, General
Headquarters USA,
Melville, New York
1988–92
Headquarters of Canal
Plus, Paris, France
1987–95
Museum of Contemporary
Art, Barcelona, Spain
1986–95
City Hall, The Hague,
Holland
1984–97
Getty Center,
Los Angeles, California
1980–83
High Museum of Art,
Atlanta, Georgia
1979–85
Museum of Decorative
Arts, Frankfurt, Germany

Morphosis

2041 Colorado Avenue,
Santa Monica,
California 90404
Phone 310 453 2247
Fax 310 829 3270
www.morphosis.com

The studio of Morphosis
was founded by Thom
Mayne and Michael
Rotondi in 1975 in Santa
Monica, California.
Since 1991 the studio has
been directed by Thom
Mayne alone.
Thom Mayne was born
in Connecticut in 1944.
He took a degree
at USC in 1968 and
a post-graduate degree
in Architecture
at Harvard GSD in 1978.
He has taught at UCLA,
Harvard, Yale,
and SCI-Arc (he was
a founding member);
currently he teaches
Architectural Design
at UCLA.

Selected Projects
1996–98
Hypo Alpe Center
Adria, Klagenfurt, Austria
1995–97
Tower of the Sun, Seoul,
Korea
1993–2000
Pomona Ranch High
School, Pomona,
California;
Diamond Ranch High
School, Los Angeles,
California
1992–96
Blades Residence,
Santa Barbara, California
1992
Yuzen Museum of the
Vintage Automobile
(design), West Hollywood,
California
1989
Park of the Arts, Pavilion
of the Theatrical Arts
(competition), Los
Angeles, California
1987–92
Crawford Residence,
Montecito, California
1987
Cancer Treatment Center,
Cedars Sinai, Beverly
Hills, California
1986
Ristorante Kate Mantilini,
Beverly Hills, California
1982
Venice III, House, Venice,
California

Eric Owen Moss

8557 Higuera Street,
Culver City,
California 90232-2535
Phone 310 839 1199
Fax 310 839 7922
E-mail
ericmoss@ix.netcom.com

Eric Owen Moss was born
in 1943 in Los Angeles,
California. He took
a degree in Literature
at UCLA in 1965,
a degree in Architecture
at the same university in
1968, and a post-graduate
degree in Architecture
at Harvard University
GSD in 1972. Since 1974
he has been a professor
of Design at SCI-Arc
in Los Angeles.
He founded the studio
of Eric Owen Moss
Architects in 1976
in Culver City, California.

Selected Projects
1997–2000
Stealth, 3535 Hayden,
Trivida Culver City,
California;
3520 Hayden, 8522
National Culver City,
California;
The Beehive, The Box
Culver City, California;
Parking Garage/
Commercial Culver City,
California;
Backslash, Slash, The
Umbrella Culver City,
California
1993–94
IRS Building, Culver City,
California
1990–96
Samitaur, Culver City,
California
1990–94
The Box, Culver City,
California
1988–90
Gary Group, Culver City,
California
1987–89
Paramount Laundry,
Culver City, California;
Lindblade Tower, Culver
City, California
1986–89
Central Housing Office,
University of California,
Irvine, California

Patkau

L110 560 Beatty Street,
Vancouver,
British Columbia
(Canada) V6B 2L3
Phone 604 683 7633
Fax 604 683 7634
www.patkau.ca

The studio of Patkau
was founded in 1978
in Edmonton, Alberta,
by Patricia Patkau and
her husband John.
In 1984 the studio moved
to Vancouver, British
Columbia.
In 1995 Michael
Cunningham became
a partner in the studio.
Patricia Patkau was born
in 1950 in Winnipeg,
Manitoba. She took a
degree in Interior Design
at Manitoba University
and a post-graduate
degree in Architecture
at Yale University. Besides
teaching at the University
of British Columbia,
Patricia Patkau has been
a visiting professor at
Harvard GSD, Yale, and
UCLA. She is currently
an associate professor
in the Department
of Architecture at the
University of British
Columbia. In 1995
she held the 'Eliot Noyes'
Chair at the GDS
at Harvard.

John Patkau was born
in 1947 in Winnipeg,
Manitoba. After taking a
degree in Art and a degree
in Environmental Studies
at Manitoba University,
he took a post-graduate
degree in Architecture at
the same university. In
1995, along with his wife
Patricia, he held the 'Eliot
Noyes' Chair at the GDS
at Harvard.

Selected Projects
1999
Campus Master Planning,
Houston, Texas
1998
Nursing and Biomedical
Sciences Building,
Houston, Texas
1997
Agosta House, San Juan
Island, Washington
1993
Whistler Library and
Museum (feasibility
study), Whistler, British
Columbia
1992
Strawberry Vale
Elementary School,
Victoria, British Columbia
1990
Newton Library, Surrey,
British Columbia
1988
Canadian Clay and Glass
Gallery, Waterloo, Ontario
1988
Seabird Island School,
Agassiz, British Columbia

1987
Greene House,
West Vancouver,
British Columbia
1984
Patkau House,
West Vancouver,
British Columbia

**Pei, Cobb, Freed
& Partners**
600 Madison Avenue,
New York, New York
10022
Phone 212 751 3122
Fax 212 872 5443
E-mail pcf@pcfandp.com /
www.pcfandp.com

The studio of Pei, Cobb,
Freed & Partners was
founded by I.M. Pei
in 1989, in New York.
Ieoh Ming Pei was born
in 1917 in Canton, now
Guangzhou, in China.
He took a degree in
Architecture in 1940
at MIT, a post-graduate
degree in 1942 at Harvard
University, and in 1946
a doctorate at the same
university. From 1945
to 1948 he taught at
the Graduate School
of Design of Harvard
University.
In 1954 he was naturalized
as an American citizen,
and in 1955 he founded
the studio I.M. Pei
& Associates.
In 1983 he was awarded
the Pritzker Prize.
Henry Cobb was born
in 1926, and took a degree
in Architecture at the
GSD of Harvard. Between
1980 and 1985 he was the
head of the Department
of Architecture at the
GSD of Harvard.

James Ingo Freed was
born in Essen, Germany,
in 1930.
He took a degree in 1953
at the Illinois Institute
of Technology (ITT) and
became an associate
in 1956 of I.M. Pei.
He was a professor
and dean of the ITT
from 1975 to 1978,
and he has taught
at the Cooper Union
and at Yale University.

Selected Projects
1992–97
Miho Shigaraki Museum,
Shiga, Japan
1989–93
United States Holocaust
Memorial Museum,
Washington, D.C.
1987–95
The Rock and Roll Hall
of Fame and Museum,
Cleveland, Ohio
1983–93
Grand Louvre, Paris,
France
1982–89
Tower of the Bank
of China, Hong Kong,
China
1980–83
Charles Shipman
Payson Building,
Portland Museum
of Art, Portland, Maine
1968–78
National Gallery of Art,
East Building,
Washington, D.C.

1965–79
John F. Kennedy Library,
Boston, Massachusetts

Cesar Pelli

1056 Chapel Street,
New Haven,
Connecticut 06510
Phone 203 777 2515
Fax 203 787 2856

Cesar Pelli was born
in Tucuman, Argentina,
in 1926, and emigrated
to the U.S. in 1952 and
was naturalized in 1964.
He took a degree in
Architecture in 1954
at the University
of Illinois.
Before opening his own
studio he was an associate
of the Studio of Eero
Saarinen and Associates
(1954 and 1964) and
a partner of Gruen
Associates (1968–76).
He founded the studio
of Cesar Pelli &
Associates in 1977 in
New Haven, Connecticut.
Cesar Pelli was the dean
of the School of
Architecture at Yale
University from 1977
to 1984.

Selected Projects
1991–97
Petronas Twin Towers,
Kuala Lumpur, Malaysia
1990–95
Building of the Central
Headquarters of NTT
Shinjuku, Tokyo,
Japan

1987–92
NationsBank Corporate
Center, Charlotte,
North Carolina
1987–91
Canary Wharf Tower,
London, England
1983–85
Four Leaf Tower,
Houston, Texas
1980–88
World Financial Center,
New York, New York
1977
Residential tower and
expansion of the Museum
of Modern Art, New
York, New York

Antoine Predock

300 12th Street NW,
Albuquerque,
New Mexico 87102
Phone 505 843 7390
Fax 505 243 6254
www.predock.com

Antoine Predock was
born in 1936 in Lebanon,
Missouri. He took
a degree in Architecture
at Columbia University
in New York, in 1962.
He founded the studio
of Antoine Predock
Architect in 1967
in Albuquerque,
New Mexico. He taught
as visiting professor
at Clemson University
in 1995, at the GSD
of Harvard in 1987,
and at Maryland
University.

Selected Projects
1999
College of Arts
and Letters Facilities,
Southwest Missouri
State University, Missouri
1998
Unità della Chiesa
Cristiana, Houston,
Texas;
Performing Arts and
Education Center, Green
Valley, Arizona;
College of Colorado,
Colorado Springs,
Colorado

1997
Mackay Residence
in Paradise Valley,
Phoenix, Arizona
1996
Teaching Museum
and Art Gallery,
Skidmore College,
Saratoga Springs,
New York
1994
Spencer Theater for
Theater Arts, Ruidoso,
New Mexico;
Center for Nanoscale
Science and Technology,
Rice University, Houston,
Texas
1991
Museum of Science and
Industry, Tampa, Florida;
Science Center, Phoenix,
Arizona
1988
Disney Hotel
Mediterraneo,
Orlando, Florida;
Hotel Santa Fe, Euro
Disney, Marne-la-Vallée,
France
1987
Los Alamos Library,
Los Alamos, New Mexico;
Museum and Central
Library, Las Vegas,
Nevada;
American Heritage
Center and Art Museum,
University of Wyoming,
Laramie, Wyoming
1982
Rio Grande Nature
Center Master Plan

& Visitor Center
Albuquerque,
New Mexico
1979
Museum of Albuquerque,
Albuquerque,
New Mexico

Ro.To. Architects

600 Moulton Avenue
#405, Los Angeles,
California
Phone 213 226 1102
Fax 213 226 1105

The studio of Ro. To.
Architects was founded
in 1993, in Los Angeles,
by Michael Rotondi
and Clark Stevens.
Michael Rotondi was born
in 1949 in Los Angeles,
California.
He took a degree
in Architecture
at Southern California
Institute of Architecture
(SCI-Arc) in 1973.
From 1976 to 1987 he
was director of the
Graduate Design Faculty
at SCI-Arc, while from
1987 he has been
director of SCI-Arc.
Between 1976 and 1991
he was a partner of Thom
Mayne in the studio
of Morphosis.
Clark Stevens worked
with the studio
of Morphosis from 1987
to 1991.

Selected Projects
1994–99
Sinte Gleska University,
Antelope, South Dakota
1993–96
Carlson-Reges Residence,
Los Angeles, California

1992–93
Ristorante Nicola,
Los Angeles, California
1990–95
Teiger House, Somerset
County, New Jersey
1989–95
Qwfk House, New Jersey

**Venturi, Scott Brown
and Associates**

4236 Main Street,
Philadelphia, Pennsylvania
19127-1696
Phone 215 487 0400
Fax 215 487 2520
www.vsba.com

The studio of Venturi,
Scott Brown and
Associates was founded
in 1961, in Philadelphia,
by the architects Robert
Venturi and Denise Scott
Brown.
Robert Venturi was born
in 1925 in Philadelphia.
He took a degree in
Literature in 1947 at
Princeton University
and also took a degree
in Architecture in 1950,
at the same university.
Between 1954 and 1956
he had a scholarship to
study at the American
Academy in Rome. Before
opening his own studio he
worked with Louis Kahn
and Eero Saarinen. He has
taught at Yale University,
the University of
Pennsylvania, the
University of California,
Princeton University,
and at Harvard GSD.
Denise Scott Brown was
born in 1931 in Nkana,
Zambia. She took a degree
in Architecture in 1955,
at the Architectural

Association of London
and, in 1960, at
Pennsylvania University
where in 1965 she took
a post-graduate degree
in Architecture. She has
taught at Pennsylvania
University, UCLA, and
at the University of
California at Berkeley.

Selected Projects
1992–99
Headquarters
of the Departement
of Haute-Garonne,
Toulouse, France
1992–97
Hotel Mielparque Resort
Complex Nikko, Kirifuri,
Japan
1992–96
Ferry Terminal, Whitehall
New York, New York;
Memorial Hall (restoration
and renovation), including
Annenberg Hall
and Loker Commons,
Harvard University,
Cambridge,
Massachusetts
1989–94
Library of Bard
College (expansion),
Annandale-on-Hudson,
New York
1989–92
Children's Museum,
Houston, Texas
1988–93
George La Vie Schultz
Laboratories,
Department of Biology,

Princeton University,
Princeton, New Jersey
1986–91
Sainsbury Wing, National
Gallery, London, England
1986–96
San Diego Contemporary
Art Museum (expansion,
renovation, and
restoration), La Jolla,
California
1985–91
Furness Building, Fisher
Library of Fine Arts
(restoration and
renovation), Philadelphia,
Pennsylvania
1985–90
Clinical Research
Building, School
of Medicine, University
of Pennsylvania,
Philadelphia, Pennsylvania

Rafael Vinoly

50 Vandam Street,
New York,
New York 10013
Phone 212 924 5060
Fax 212 924 5858

Rafael Vinoly was born
in Montevideo,
Uruguay. He took
a degree in Architecture
in 1969,
in the Department
of Architecture at the
University of Buenos
Aires, where he taught
Architectural Design.
He came to the United
States in 1978; Vinoly
taught at the University
of Washington and
in the School of Design
at Harvard University.
In 1979 he moved
permanently to New York,
and he has taught
at Harvard University,
Yale University,
the Rhode Island
School of Design,
Pennsylvania University,
Columbia University,
and the Institute
of Architecture
of Southern California.
Currently the studio
of Rafael Vinoly
Architects, founded
in 1983 in New York,
also has offices in Tokyo,
Buenos Aires,
and London.

Selected Projects
1998
Palmer Stadium,
Princeton, New Jersey;
Samsung World Pulse
Headquarters, Seoul,
Korea
1989–96
Tokyo International
Forum, Tokyo, Japan
1989
NYNEX, New York,
New York
1985
Manhattan
Condominiums-East/West
Towers, New York,
New York
1978
Mendoza Sports Complex,
Buenos Aires, Argentina
1968
Bank of the City of
Buenos Aires, Buenos
Aires, Argentina

**Williams, Tsien
and Associates**

222 Central Park South,
New York, New York
10019
Phone 212 582 2385
Fax 212 245 1984
E-mail mail@twbta.com
www.twbta.com

The studio of Williams,
Tsien and Associates was
founded in New York in
1986 by the architects Tod
Williams and Billie Tsien.
Tod Williams was born in
1943 in Detroit, Michigan.
He took a degree in Fine
Arts in 1965, at Princeton
University, and a post-
graduate degree in
Architecture in 1967,
at the same university.
Since the early Seventies
he has taught at many
American universities,
including: the Cooper
Union in New York from
1973 to 1989, Harvard
University GSD in 1987,
the Institute of
Architecture of Southern
California from 1987 to
1989, the University
of Virginia in 1990, and
Yale University in 1992.
In 1998, with his wife
Billie Tsien, he was
awarded the 'Jane
and Bruce Graham'
Chair at the University
of Pennsylvania

Billie Tsien was born in
1949 at Ithaca, New York.
She took a degree
in Fine Arts in 1971
at Yale University and
a post-graduate degree
in Architecture in 1977,
at UCLA. Since 1986 she
has taught at the Institute
of Architecture of
Southern California,
Parsons University,
Yale University, Harvard
University GSD,
and University of Texas
at Austin.

Selected Projects
1999
Sports Center
at Cranbrook, Bloomfield
Hills, Michigan
1998–2001
Museum of American
Folk Art, New York,
New York
1996
Emma Willard School:
Science Building
and Natatorium,
Troy, New York;
Phoenix Art Museum,
Phoenix, Arizona
1995
Neurological Institute,
La Jolla, California
1993
Single-Family House,
New York, New York
1992
New College of the
University of Virginia,
Charlottesville, Virginia

1986
Feinberg Hall, Princeton,
New Jersey

Bibliographies

Asymptote

Cathy Lang Ho,
'Computer Power',
in *Architecture*, May 2000,
pp. 156–61.

Luca Molinari,
'Guggenheim irreale',
in *Ventiquattro*, no. 3,
June 2000, pp. 91–94.

Hani Rashid,
'Guggenheim Virtual
Museum', in *Domus*,
January 2000, pp. 27–31.

Various authors,
'The Advanced Trading
Floor Operations Center
in the NYSE', in *Domus*,
June 1999, pp. 39–46.

Various authors,
'Asymptote: Rashid
+ Couture', in *A+U*,
no. 344, May 1999,
pp. 22–37.

Jessie Scanlon, 'Ride
the Dow', in *Wired*,
June 1999, pp. 176–79.

TransArchitecture 03,
exhibition catalogue,
Aedes Galerie, Berlin,
1998, p. 16.

Aaron Betsky, 'Machine
Dreams', in *Architecture*,
June 1997, pp. 89–91.

Various authors, 'Univers
Theatre', in *A+U*,
no. 323, 1997, pp. 10–23.

Deborah Faush, 'The
Opposition of Modern
Tectonics', in *ANY*, 1996,
pp. 48–57.

Various authors,
*Architecture at the
Interval, Asymptote:
Rashid + Couture*,

Rizzoli International,
monographic work, 1995.

Various authors, 'Analog
Space to Digital Field:
Asymptote Seven
Projects', in *Assemblage*,
no. 21, 1993, pp. 22–43.

Hani Rashid, 'Optigraphs
and other Writings',
in *AD Profile*, no. 89,
1991, pp. 86–91.

Various authors, 'Hani
Rashid, Lise Anne
Couture', in *A+U*,
no. 231, December 1989,
pp. 5–28.

William P. Bruder

Philip Jodidio, *Building
a New Millennium*,
Cologne, Taschen, 1999.

Oscar Riera Ojeda (edited
by), *Phoenix Central
Library, bruder DWL
architects*, Gloucester
(Mass.), Rockport
Publishers, 1999.

Richard Ingersoll,
'Le rocce del deserto',
in *Lotus*, no. 97, 1998,
pp. 24–37.

Effie Mac Donald, 'Rustic
Regionalism', in *The
Architectural Review*,
no. 1216, June 1998,
pp. 69–71.

'William P. Bruder',
in *A+U*, no. 321, June
1997.

William Curtis, 'Objet,
trame, topographie',
in *L'Architecture
d'aujourd'hui*, no. 307,
October 1996, pp. 74–87.

David Leclerc, 'Un Junkie

de l'architecture',
in *L'Architecture
d'aujourd'hui*, no. 307,
October 1996, pp. 88–95.

Peter Eisenman

Peter Eisenman, *Blurred
Zones: Works and Projects
1988-1998*, New York,
Monacelli Press, 2001.

Various authors, 'Peter
Eisenman', in *El Croquis*,
no. 85, Madrid 1997.

Cynthia C. Davidson
(edited by), *Eleven
Authors in Search of
a Building*, New York,
Monacelli Press, 1996.

Antonino Saggio,
Peter Eisenman, Rome,
Universale di architettura,
1996.

Various authors,
Eisenman Architects,
Sidney, Images
Publishing, 1995.

Jean-François Bédard
(edited by), *Cities
of Artificial Excavation,
The Work of Peter
Eisenman,1978-1988*,
New York, Rizzoli, 1994.

Pippo Ciorra, *Peter
Eisenman*, Milan, Electa,
1993.

Frank O. Gehry

Cristina Bechtler (edited
by), *Art and Architecture
in Discussion: Frank O.
Gehry / Kurt W. Forster*,
Ostfildern, Cantz Verlag,
1999.

Mildred Friedman
(edited by), *Gehry Talks:
Architecture + Process*,

New York, Rizzoli, 1999.

Francesco Dal Co,
Kurt W. Forster, *Frank
O. Gehry, The Complete
Work*, Milan, Electa,
1998.

Coosje Van Bruggen,
*Frank O. Gehry:
Guggenheim Museum
of Bilbao*, New York, The
Solomon R. Guggenheim
Foundation, 1997.

Cecilia F. Marquez
(edited by), 'Frank
O. Gehry: 1991-1995',
in *El Croquis*, no. 74/75,
Madrid, December 1995.

Yukio Futagawa, 'Frank
O. Gehry', in *GA
Architect*, no. 10,
Tokyo, 1993.

Various authors, *Frank
Gehry: New Bentwood
Furniture Designs*,
Montreal, The Montreal
Museum of Decorative
Arts, 1992.

Cecilia F. Marquez
(edited by), 'Frank
O. Gehry', in *El Croquis*,
no. 45, Madrid,
October/November,
1990.

Mildred Friedman
(edited by), *The
Architecture of Frank
Gehry*, New York, Rizzoli,
1986.

Peter Arnell, Ted
Bickford, *Frank Gehry,
Buildings and Projects*,
New York, Rizzoli, 1985.

**Gwathmey, Siegel
& Associates Architects**

Brad Collins (edited by),

243

Gwathmey and Siegel: Buildings and Projects 1965-2000, New York, Universe Publishing, 2000.

Brad Collins (edited by), *Gwathmey and Siegel Houses*, New York, Monacelli Press, 2000.

Various authors, *Gwathmey and Siegel,* Sidney, Images Publishing, 1998.

Brad Collins (edited by), *Gwathmey and Siegel: Buildings and Projects 1984-1992*, New York, Rizzoli, 1993.

Peter Arnell, Ted Bickford (edited by), *Charles Gwathmey and Robert Siegel: Buildings and Projects 1964-1984*, New York, Harper and Row, 1984.

Stanley Abercrombie, *Gwathmey and Siegel*, New York, Whitney Publ., 1981.

Steven Holl

Various authors, *The Chapel of St. Ignatius*, New York, Princeton Architectural Press, 1999.

Richard Ingersoll, 'Between Typology and Fetish', in *Architecture*, March 1999, pp. 80–89.

Various authors, 'Steven Holl', in *El Croquis*, no. 93, Madrid 1999.

Various authors, 'Steven Holl: Residence and Retreat', in *GA Houses*, no. 55, Tokyo 1998, pp. 68–75.

Richard Ingersoll, 'Holl's Northern Lights', in *Architecture*, January 1998, pp. 76–81.

Various authors, *Interwining: Selected Projects 1989-1995*, New York, Princeton Architectural Press, 1996.

Various authors, *Steven Holl architects*, New York, Monacelli Press, 1996.

Various authors, 'Questions of Perceptions. Phenomenology of Architecture', in *A+U*, Tokyo, July 1994, pp. 39–42, 121–35.

Frederic Migayron (edited by), *Steven Holl: Building and Projects*, Basel, Birkhauser, 1993.

Various authors, *Steven Holl*, New York, Rizzoli, 1993.

Steven Holl, *Anchoring: Selected Projects 1975-1988*, New York, Princeton Architecural Press, 1989.

Machado and Silvetti & Associates

Paolo Bercah, Tito Canella, 'Machado, Silvetti and the Battery', in *Zodiac*, no. 20, June 1999, pp. 64–93.

Reed Kroloff, 'Machado and Silvetti Get Real', in *Architecture*, April 1997, pp. 2–3, 80–91.

Clifford Pearson, 'Wagner Park', in *Architectural Record*, February 1997, pp. 64–69.

Rodolfo Machado, Rodolphe el-Khoury (edited by), *Monolithic Architecture*, Munich, Prestel Verlag, 1995.

Michael K. Hays (edited by), *Unprecedented Realism: The Architecture of Machado and Silvetti*, New York, Princeton Architectural Press, 1995.

Fares El-Dahdah, 'The Folly of S/M, recto verso', in *Assemblage*, no. 18, August 1992, pp. 7–19.

Peter G. Rowe, *Rodolfo Machado and Jorge Silvetti: Buildings for Cities*, New York, Rizzoli, 1989.

Various authors, 'Special Features: Works of Machado and Silvetti', in *A+U*, Tokyo, April 1990, pp. 65–138.

Richard Meier

Various authors, *Richard Meier Architect*, New York, Rizzoli, 1999.

Yukio Futagawa (edited by), *Richard Meier*, GA Document Extra 08, 1997.

Flagge Ingeborg, Oliver Hamm (edited by), *Richard Meier in Europe*, Berlin, Ernst & Sohn, 1997.

Philip Jodidio, *Richard Meier*, Cologne, Taschen, 1996.

Werner Blaser, *Richard Meier Details*, Basel, Birkhauser Verlag, 1996.

Silvio Cassarà, *Richard Meier*, Bologna, Zanichelli Editore, 1995.

Lois Nesbitt, *Richard Meier: Sculpture 1992-1994*, New York, Rizzoli, 1994.

Pippo Ciorra (edited by), *Richard Meier*, Milan, Electa, 1993.

Morphosis

Various authors, *Morphosis: Building and Projects 1993-97*, New York, Rizzoli, 1998.

Richard Weinstein, *Morphosis, Building and Projects 1989-92*, New York, Rizzoli, 1994.

Various authors, *Morphosis*, Gingko Press, 1994.

Thom Mayne, *Tangents and Outtakes: Morphosis*, New York, Rizzoli, 1993.

Richard Weinstein (edited by), *Morphosis Building and Projects*, New York, Rizzoli, 1990.

Peter Cook, George Rand, *Morphosis, Building and Projects*, New York, Rizzoli, 1989.

Carolyn Krause (edited by), *Morphosis: Architectural Projects,*

USA, The Contemporary Art Center, 1989.

Eric Owen Moss

Various authors, *Eric Owen Moss. Planet Architecture*, Los Angeles, IN.D., 2000.

James Steele (edited by), *PS: a Building by Eric Owen Moss*, Sidney, Images Publishing, 1999.

Eric Owen Moss, *Gnostic Architecture*, New York, Monacelli Press, 1998.

Brad Collins, *Eric Owen Moss. Buildings and Projects 2*, New York, Rizzoli, 1996.

'Owen Moss, Eric, 1974-1994', in *A+U*, November 1994.

Various authors, *Eric Owen Moss: The Box*, New York, Princeton University Press, 1994.

James Steele, *Eric Owen Moss*, Architectural Monographs No. 29, London, Academy Editions, 1993.

Various authors, *Eric Owen Moss*, Architectural Monographs No. 20, London, Academy Editions, 1993.

Various authors, *Eric Owen Moss, Buildings and Projects*, New York, Rizzoli, 1991.

Patkau

'Patkau, Vancouver House, Agosta House',

in *GA Houses*, March 2000, pp. 42–47.

'Poetic Pragmatism', in *The Architectural Review*, December 1999, pp. 88–91.

Brian Carter, 'Canadian Club', in *The Architectural Review,* August 1999, pp. 57–59.

Ruggero Lenci, 'Architetture Senza Capriata', in *L'Architettura*, no. 524, June 1999, pp. 346–68.

Patkau, Patricia, *Technology Place & Architecture*, in Kenneth Frampton (edited by), *The Jerusalem Seminar in Architecture,* New York, Rizzoli, 1998, pp. 94–111.

Antonella Mari, 'Newton Library, Surrey', in *Domus*, June 1998, pp. 34–39.

Various authors, *Patkau Architects,* Barcelona, Gustavo Gili, 1997.

Brian Carter, 'Strawbery Vale', in *The Architectural Review* , no. 1206, August 1997, pp. 34–41.

Kenneth Frampton, 'Tecto-Totemic Form', in *Perspecta*, no. 28, 1997, pp. 180–89.

'Strawberry Vale School, Victoria, British Columbia', in *Domus*, no. 789, January 1997, pp. 8–15.

Lynnette Widder, 'Room Constituted by Topography:

on Vancouver Island',
in *Daidalos*, no. 63,
March 1997, pp. 116–21.

Sandy Isenstadt,
Spectacular Tectonics,
in 'ANY', no. 14, 1996,
pp. 44–47.

Aaron Betsky, 'Romantic
Realism', in *Architectural
Record*, no. 183, January
1995, pp. 64–69.

Brian Carter (edited by),
*Patkau Architects, Selected
Projects 1983-93*, Halifax,
Nova Scotia, Tuns Press,
1994.

Kenneth Frampton,
'L'America incognita:
un'antologia / America
Incognito: An Anthology',
in *Casabella*, December
1993, pp. 51, 54,
62–63, 70.

John and Patricia Patkau,
*Canadian Clay and Glass
Gallery, Vision to Reality,
1981-93*, exhibition
catalogue, Waterloo
(Ontario), Canadian
Clay and Glass Gallery,
1993.

Brian Carter (edited by),
*The Canadian Clay and
Glass Gallery: The Act
of Transformation*,
Halifax, Nova Scotia,
Tuns Press, 1992.

Trevor Boddy, 'Pacific
Patkau', in *The
Architectural Review*,
no. 1134, August 1991,
pp. 32–38.

Adele Freedman, John
and Patricia Patkau,
*Sight Lines: Looking
at Architecture and Design
in Canada*, Ontario,

Oxford University Press,
1990, pp. 88–91.

Various authors, *Patkau
Architects: Projects
1978-1990*, Vancouver,
UBC Fine Arts Gallery,
1990.

**Pei, Cobb, Freed
& Partners**

I.M. Pei, *Light
is the Key*, Germany,
Prestel Publ., 2000.

Various authors, *Readings
on I.M. Pei*, Taipei,
Huang Jian Min, 1999.

Michael Cannell, *I.M. Pei:
Mandarin of Modernism*,
New York, Carol
Southern Books, 1995.

James Steele (edited by),
Museum Builders,
London, Academy
Editions, 1994,
pp. 172–87.

Carter Wiseman, *I.M. Pei:
a Profile in American
Architecture*, New York,
Harry N. Abrams, 1990.

Bruno Suner, *Pei*, Paris,
Hazan, 1988.

Peter Blake, 'I.M. Pei
e Partners',
in *Architecture Plus*,
February 1973,
pp. 52–59; March 1973,
pp. 20–77.

Cesar Pelli

Cesar Pelli, *Observations
for Young Architects*,
New York, Monacelli
Press, 1999.

Various authors, *Cesar
Pelli Recent Themes*,

Boston, Birkhauser, 1999.
David Anger, *Cesar Pelli*,
Capstone Press, 1995.

Various authors,
Cesar Pelli and Associates,
vol. I, Australia, Images
Publishing, 1994.

Various authors,
Cesar Pelli, Sidney,
Images Publishing, 1993.

Various authors,
*Cesar Pelli, Buildings
and Projects 1965-1990*,
New York, Rizzoli,
1990.

John Pastier, *Cesar
Pelli*, New York,
Elliot's Book, 1980.

Antoine Predock

Various authors,
Antoine Predock,
Barcelona, Gustavo Gili,
1999.

Various authors,
*Antoine Predock
Architect, Monograph II*,
New York, Rizzoli,
1998.

Geoffrey Baker,
Antoine Predock, London,
Architectural Monograph
No. 49, Academy
Editions, 1997.

Various authors,
*One House Series:
Turtle Creek House*,
New York, Monacelli
Press, 1997.

Alan Hess, *Hyperwest*,
New York, Watson
Guptill Publications,
1996.

Brad Collins, Juliette
Robbins (edited by),

*Antoine Predock
Architect*, New York,
Rizzoli Monograph,
1994.

Ro.To. Architects

'Ro.To. architects.
Università Sinte
Gleska', in *Casabella*,
no. 679, June 2000,
pp. 62–79.

Sarah Amelar, 'Project
diary', in *Architectural
Record*, November 1999,
pp. 85–93.

Joseph Giovannini,
'Powered Up',
in *Architecture*, no. 57,
February 1998,
pp. 64–73.

Wendy Moonan,
'A Mathematical
Ordering System Helped
Ro.To. Architects Sculpt
a Complex Scheme',
in *Architectural Record*,
April 1997.

Paul Goldberger,
'Michael Rotondi,
A Contemporary Villa
Embraces the New
Jersey Landscape',
in *Architectural Digest*,
March 1997.

Enrico Morteo,
'Architettura
dell'orientamento',
in *Abitare*, no. 362,
May 1997.

Fujii Wayne, 'Ro.To.
Architects', in *GA
Houses*, no. 51,
April 1997, pp. 46–69.

Michael Rotondi,
'Impossibile da finire',
in *Lotus*, no. 77,
June 1993.

**Venturi, Scott Brown
and Associates**

Writings by Robert
Venturi and Denise Scott
Brown

Robert Venturi,
*Iconography and
Electronics upon a Generic
Architecture. A View
from the Drafting
Room*, Cambridge
(Mass.), MIT Press, 1996.

Robert Venturi, Denise
Scott Brown, Steve
Izenour, *Learning from
Las Vegas*, Cambridge
(Mass.), MIT Press,
1972.

Robert Venturi,
*Complexity and
Contradiction in
Architecture*, New York,
Museum of Modern Art,
1966.

Writings on the Work
of Robert Venturi
and Denise Scott Brown

Carolina Vaccaro
(edited by), *Venturi Scott
Brown. Maniera del
moderno*, Bari, Editori
Laterza, 2000.

Stanislaus von Moos,
*Venturi Scott Brown &
Associates 1986-1998*,
New York, Monacelli
Press, 1999.

Amedeo Belluzzi, *Venturi,
Scott Brown e Associati*,
Bari, Editori Laterza,
1992.

C. Vaccaro, F. Schwartz
(edited by), *Venturi Scott
Brown e Associati*,
Bologna, Zanichelli
Editore, 1991.

Stanislaus von Moos,
*Venturi, Rauch & Scott
Brown. Buildings and
Projects*, New York,
Monacelli Press,
1986.

A. di Sanmartin (edited
by), *Venturi, Rauch
& Scott Brown. Obras
y proyectos 1959-1985*,
Barcelona, Gustavo
Gili, 1987.

'Venturi et Rauch.
Projects et travaux
récentes',
in *L'Architecture
d'aujourd'hui*, no. 197,
June 1978.

Various authors, *Venturi
and Rauch. The Public
Buildings*, London,
Thames and Hudson,
1978.

Rafael Vinoly

'Vinoly Defies Convention
in Pittsburgh',
in *Architecture*,
April 1999.

Various authors,
*Contemporary World
Architecture*, London,
Phaidon Press, 1998.

Various authors, *Veinte
Obras de la ultima decada
en el Museo Nacional de
Bellas Artes*, exhibition
catalogue, Buenos Aires,
1998.

'Rafael Vinoly Princeton
Stadium', in *Architecture*,
November 1998.

W. Le Cuyer (edited by),
*Rafael Vinoly-The Making
of Public Space*, John
Dinkeloo Memorial
Lecture, 1997.

'The Future, Tokyo International Forum', in *The Architectural Review*, November 1996.

'Tokyo International Forum', in *Architecture*, October 1996.

'Il Progetto del Tokyo International Forum', in *Casabella*, July-August 1995.

'Lo Spazio Simbolico: the Tokyo International Forum', in *L'Arca*, February, July-August 1994.

Herbert Muschamp, 'Vinoly's Vision for Tokyo and for the Identity of Japan', in *The New York Times*, 16 July 1992.

'Tokyo International Forum', in *A+U*, 1990.

'John Jay College', in *A+U*, 1989.

'Houses in La Lucila, Province of Buenos Aires, Argentina, 1969-71', in *GA Houses*, July, 1984.

Williams, Tsien and Associates

Various authors, *Williams and Tsien: Work/Life*, New York, Monacelli Press, 2000.

Various authors, *Williams Tsien. Obras/ Works*, 2G, No. 9, Barcelona, Gustavo Gili, 1999.

Joan Oackman, 'Tod Williams e Billie Tsien, casa a Manhattan', in *Casabella*, no. 642, February 1997.

Pat Morton, 'Il paesaggio della mediazione, il nuovo college, University of Virginia', in *Casabella*, no. 610, pp. 58–67.

Douglas Heller, *Tod Williams, Billie Tsien and Associates*, New York, Sage Publications, 1992.

Douglas Heller, *Tod Williams Billie Tsien and Associates: An Annotated Bibliography*, Chicago, Illinois, Council of Planning Librarians, 1992.

'Interview: Tod Williams and Billie Tsien', in *Progressive Architecture*, no. 5, May 1990, pp. 119–20.